Happy Hound

Develop a Great Relationship with Your Adopted Dog or Puppy

Susan C. Daffron
Logical Expressions, Inc.

ISBN-13: 978-0-9749245-2-6

ISBN-10: 0-9749245-2-0

Library of Congress Control Number: 2006909898

Warning and disclaimer: This book is designed to provide information
about adopting and caring for dogs. Every effort has been made to make
it as complete and accurate as possible, but no warranty or fitness is
implied.

The information in this book is provided on an "as is" basis. Logical
Expressions, Inc. and the author take no responsibility for any errors or
omissions. The author and Logical Expressions, Inc. also shall have no
responsibility to any person or entity with respect to loss or damages
arising from information contained in this book or from any programs or
documents that may accompany it.

Contents

Adopting a Dog 1

   About Me 2

   Every Rescue Has a Story 3

   Why Adopt a Dog? 8

      Pets and Us 9

   Is Adoption Right for You? 11

      Time and Patience 11

      Should You Get a Dog? 12

      Choosing a Breed 13

      Breed Checklist 15

   Acquiring a Dog 16

      Adopting from a Shelter 17

      Breed Rescue 18

      The Darker Side of "Rescue" 19

      Parking Lot Pups 20

      Finder's Keepers 21

      A Puppy for Christmas? 22

      Dog Personality Tests 23

Bringing Your Dog Home 27

   The First Days 27

      Essential Dog Supplies 27

      More on Collars 29

      Dog Beds 30

      Bonding with Your Rescued Dog 31

      Happy Spay Day 33

      Early Age Spay/Neuter 34

The Mythical Miracle..35

Adjusting to the Family 36

    Canine and Feline Cohabitation...........................37

    Kids and Pets...38

    Retaining Pack Harmony 39

    Dog Group Names 42

Understanding Your Dog...*43*

Be Leader of Your Pack..43

Dog Body Language 45

    Mad Ears 47

Canine Communication 48

    The Mighty Woo 50

Walk the Dog...51

Educating Your Dog *53*

Socializing Your Dog..54

Nip Mouthing..56

Preventing Dog Bites..57

Training...59

    Learning Manners..59

    Dog Training Tips..60

    Dog Training Misconceptions 61

    Positive Reinforcement..62

    The Power of Positive Reinforcement 63

    The Value of "No" 65

    Teach Your Dog to Sit...67

    The Sit Stomp...69

    Stay vs. Okay...70

    Teach Your Dog to Stay Down.............................71

    Teach Your Dog to Come When Called...............73

Teach Your Dog to Walk on a Leash.................................75

No, I Will Not Go 78

Teach "Go to Your Bed" 79

Housebreaking...80

The Basic Principles 81

Housebreaking Schedules..82

Deal with Mistakes...83

Cleaning Up "Accidents" 84

More on Crate Training 85

Dealing with Behavior Problems **89**

Providing Structure for Insecure Dogs........................89

Sometimes Dog Problems are People Problems.................91

Think About the Pets 92

Canine Teen Rebellion...94

Jumping Dogs 95

You Must Chill..96

Behavior: The Good, The Bad, and the Really Bad 98

Running Dogs 99

Be a Good Neighbor...100

Dealing with Escape Artists...101

Finding Your Dog..102

Dealing with a Shy Dog 104

Submissive Urination 105

Barking Dogs 107

Digging Dogs 108

Marking..109

Fear of Loud Noises...110

Thunder Paws 113

Destructive Chewing..114

Dog Aggression 115

What to Do About Dogs that Eat
Non-Edible Things (Pica) 117

    Canine Murphy's Law.. 119

Licking Dogs 120

Keeping Your Dog Healthy *123*

    Grooming 123

        Dealing with Mats 124

        Washing Your Dog 126

        Full Body Shake... 128

        Stink Dawg 129

        Canine Pedicure... 130

        The Ears Have It.. 131

        The Houseguests You Don't Want 132

        Hair, Hair Everywhere 134

        The GURP 136

    Health Care 137

        Choosing a Vet.. 137

        Pets Need Physicals Too..................................... 139

        Help Your Vet Help Your Dog............................ 141

        Fat Dogs.. 143

        Why Vaccinate 144

        Boarding and Bordetella 145

        Doggie Dental Care... 146

        Post Surgical Pet Care.. 148

        Miss Cone Head.. 150

        Heartworm Disease.. 151

        Bloat 152

        Canine Pancreatitis 153

        Arthritis... 155

Canine Epilepsy and Seizures 156

Licking, Biting, and Chewing.. 158

Endless Slurping 160

Keeping Your Dog Safe...***161***

Puppy Proofing... 161

Poisonous Outdoor Plants 162

Antifreeze.. 163

Hot Weather Tips 164

The Bear Pool 166

Have a Safe Fourth... 167

Get Your Dog Ready for Winter 168

The Wood Stove Incident 169

Do You Need to Winterize Your Dog?............................. 170

Tender Toes 172

Holiday Treats Your Dog Shouldn't Eat 173

Pet Proofing the Holidays.. 174

Tannenbaum Bomb.. 177

Dog FAQ...***179***

Why Do Dogs Chase Their Tails?..................................... 179

How Old is Your Dog? 180

Do Dogs Dream?... 182

Why Do Dogs Eat Grass? 184

How Can I Have a Dog and a Job Too?............................ 185

Top 10 Reasons Dogs are Better Office
Mates than Humans... 187

What is The "Human–Animal Bond"? 188

How Can I Say Goodbye?... 190

It's All Worth It.. 191

Adopting a Dog

This book is about many things. It's about how to prepare for dog adoption, how to choose the right dog for you, and how to deal with all the challenges that go hand in hand with owning and loving a shelter dog. Yet underpinning all these topics is an even more important idea: reality.

For me, the reality of developing a lifetime relationship with an adopted dog is one of the most emotionally satisfying activities on the planet. You don't read about this kind of dog–human bond in most training or dog care books, which often sound like manuals in programming the perfect, "pushbutton" canine.

This book takes a more realistic approach. It's all about finding, nurturing, and relating to a hound you can happily live with for a lifetime, even if that hound isn't the model of purebred beauty or obedience trial behavior.

During the years I've worked in animal shelters and veterinary offices, written about dogs and cats, and raised my own shelter pets, I've learned that perfection isn't just unimportant, it's also impractical. In spite of what so many books claim, in the real world there are no "perfect" dogs. There are only imperfectly wonderful, wacky, charming, cute, heroic, and loving dogs, and the equally imperfect humans who love them.

For every slick, textbook-trained canine "robot," there are thousands of imperfectly glorious human–dog relationships. Sure, the basics need to be there: no biting, no going to the bathroom in the house, no destruction of objects or people. Those are the foundations of civilized coexistence, and this book addresses all those issues thoroughly.

But once you get beyond the basics, this book is mostly about care, communication, and understanding. All relationships depend on trade-offs, so in this book you'll find plenty of real-world guidance about how to decide which house rules and doggie behaviors are non-negotiable.

In the end, you might be one of those people who are horrified when their hound jumps on the sofa, but will gladly allow Rover to climb into bed with you at night. Or you might decide that all human furniture is off limits, yet you happily let your dog drag you for miles on long hikes. Neither scenario is perfect, but who cares? Whatever works. If you and your dog are happy, healthy, safe, and love each other in spite of the imperfections, everything is fine.

This book is dedicated to you and your adopted dog. May you enjoy your imperfections and be happy together for years to come!

About Me

This book is designed especially for owners of dogs that have been adopted from humane societies, animal shelters, or breed rescues. It's about dogs that have been given a second chance at a new home, so I don't talk about the latest in "showing dogs" or "breeding to type." There's no snob factor here; plenty of books exist for breed enthusiasts. Instead, this book is for people who want to develop a good relationship with their family dog.

As a former animal shelter volunteer, veterinary technician, and owner of six shelter critters, I've seen a lot. This book contains my best advice for people like you, who have chosen to adopt, but need specialized guidance on dealing with "previously owned" dogs.

This book also includes my personal experiences in solving the problems of my own adopted canines. I've helped them through the entire spectrum of post-pet-adoption woes and I've explained them in sidebars that appear throughout the book. The sidebars also contain a few personal reflections on life with weirdly wonderful happy hounds.

With four dogs, I have lived through and found solutions for the following problems: separation anxiety, barking, submissive urination, excitement urination, jumping on people, destructive chewing, digging, and many other horrible things that I've probably blocked from my memory. Are my dogs perfect? No. Am I an extraordinary pet owner? No. I'm just like you— someone who likes dogs and enjoys their fuzzy presence in my world.

However, I do realize that every pet is an individual and you have to work within the limitations of the animal's personality. My dog Cami, for example, had numerous behavior problems. We've worked through a lot of them, but she is always going to be a shy dog and as such, she's not fond of new people or places. She is a creature of routine. (I can think of a few people like that too!)

My dogs' behavior and medical problems have often stumped me. But I found answers, which I share here with you. If you've ever read a dog book that sounded like it was written by someone who has never owned a dog, rest assured, this book is different. I helped my dogs with myriad problems, and now they are joys to be around. If I can do it, so can you!

Every Rescue Has a Story

Because I refer to my own animals throughout this book, it's probably good to start with a few introductions. You'll find caricatures of my critters in the sidebars, so here I give you photos of the real live dogs, along with my rendition.

When I worked at an animal shelter, I learned that every rescue has a story. So without further ado, meet the all-furry team!

Leia (Black Border Collie Mix) About a month after moving to Idaho, I started volunteering at the local animal shelter. There I met a fuzzy little black pup who wasn't healthy. She also had the disadvantage of being a black puppy and getting older. As shelter workers will attest, black dogs often are harder to adopt. Suffice it to say, no one wanted this dirty, somewhat sickly pup. The folks at the shelter said she either had kennel cough or distemper. I decided I didn't want that little black pup to lose her chance at a home, so I adopted Leia, and took her to the vet.

The problem turned out to be kennel cough and a few antibiotics later, as you can see, Leia is a happy, healthy hound. Her main vice was separation anxiety. In other words, when we left her alone, she tried to eat her way out of the house. We tried many things, but basically the best thing we did was get Tika. We always say that Tika is Leia's dog, and it's true.

Tika (Golden Retriever)
Tika's story starts off badly. She began her life as a puppy mill puppy. When the mill was raided in the winter of 1997, she was dumped in the street and found with her feet frozen into the ice by an elderly couple in downtown Sandpoint, Idaho, about 30 miles away from the puppy mill. Tika was about 6 weeks old at the time and her medical records said she was "immunosuppressed." But the older couple took her in and put her in the back yard. Unfortunately, by the time Tika was 5 months old the couple couldn't take her hyperactive ways anymore and brought her to the animal shelter.

When I adopted Tika, she had almost every behavior problem in the book. Submissive urination, excitement urination, jumping on people, you name it. She couldn't focus on anything long enough to even begin to be trained. Suffice it to say, Tika was completely out of control. My husband James couldn't touch her for the first 6 months we had her. After consulting with a behaviorist and vets, I discovered that Tika is hyperkinetic (the doggie equivalent of ADHD in kids), a situation that has been resolved through obedience classes and behavior modification training.

Cami (White Samoyed/Aussie Shepherd/Lab Mix)

Cami was the cutest puppy I had ever seen. (And as an animal shelter volunteer and employee, I have seen a LOT of puppies.) When I was volunteering at the shelter, I spent some time holding and cuddling her. After I got home, I told my husband about the tiny adorable fuzz ball puppy I'd met. When I showed Cami to James, it was love at first sight. He cuddled Cami and couldn't leave the building without her.

Cami was well adjusted, until she hit 4 months old. Then she became psycho weirdo dog. I thought I knew about dogs, but I couldn't figure her out. No one else could either. After three years filled with vet trips, veterinary university consultations, medications, and socialization classes, I ran across a reference to a study indicating that thyroid imbalance can affect canine behavior. So I had the vet do a "full thyroid panel" and, lo and behold, Cami's problems were because of a lack of thyroid hormones! Now with her daily thyroid supplements, Cami is a happy, healthy little hound again.

Leto (Off-White Great Pyrenees/Retriever Mix)
The big boy's story is a tale of travels. Originally, Leto was picked up as a stray in Los Angeles, California. Because he was white (sort of), the shelter called Samoyed rescue. He looks nothing like a Samoyed, but because he was SO nice, the rescue folks took him anyway. He went to foster care in Temecula, CA, and then later Redding, CA. Meanwhile, because of Cami's myriad mysterious behavior problems, I had subscribed to an online Samoyed discussion list, SamFans (http://www.samfans.org). The link to Leto's picture was posted and I saw it and fell in love with his gentle brown eyes. After much email discussion and applying for adoption, the task of getting him to Idaho presented itself. Enter the Canine Underground Railroad, a network of volunteers who drive dogs to their "forever" homes.

All told, Leto went from the Lancaster (LA County) shelter to Murrieta, CA: 120 miles; Murrieta to Redding, CA: 325 miles; Redding, CA to Vancouver, WA: 430 miles; Vancouver to Seattle, WA: 164 miles; then Seattle, WA to somewhat north of Sandpoint, Idaho: 400 miles. For a grand total of 1439 miles! When I got him, he was extremely skinny and after months of the "good life" here in Idaho, he still wasn't putting on weight. After conventional medicine failed, I cured his digestive problems through more alternative means.

Why Adopt a Dog?

Obviously there are many more dogs out there than there are permanent, loving homes for them. Recent pet care industry studies estimate that there are 60 million dogs in the U.S. Yet only about 30 percent of puppies spend their lives with their original owner. That adds up to a lot of dogs who will eventually be sold, abandoned, or wind up in animal shelters.

The best reason for adopting a dog is to save a life. Staggering numbers of dogs are euthanized every year, and most of these are not "bad" dogs. They're not mean, dangerous, crippled, or sick. They're just unwanted and unlucky. If you've decided to make a dog a part of your life, choosing to adopt means you're going to give a dog another chance at a good life.

If you need another excellent reason to adopt, consider this: you'll be lessening the amount of animal suffering in the world. More than 80 percent of the people who give up their dogs for adoption say they just don't have time for a dog. What that really means is they never anticipated the responsibility of pet ownership. Because of their lack of foresight, the dog is taken to a shelter and his whole world is turned upside-down. When you adopt, you restore happiness and love to that critter's life, which is definitely something to feel good about!

When you adopt a dog, you'll also be doing a good deed for your community. There are financial as well as emotional costs associated with tracking down cases of animal cruelty, impounding unwanted or abused dogs, and maintaining an animal shelter. When you adopt a shelter dog, you help to ease those financial and emotional burdens.

In fact, let's look at one of the biggest challenges facing animal shelters today: pet overpopulation. Every shelter braces for the annual spring onslaught of unwanted puppies and kittens.

Shelter employees hear just about every excuse in the book for people dropping off their pet's "accidental" litters at the back door. The reason this problem continues is obvious: unlike people, cats and dogs don't have just one offspring at a time. One cat or dog who has babies and whose babies have babies can be responsible for the birth of 50 to 200 kittens or puppies in just one year. The reproductive rate of dogs is 15 times that of humans, and the reproductive rate of cats is 30 times that of humans.

Spaying or neutering is the solution to this pet overpopulation problem. It's better for you, better for the community, and (contrary to the endless old wives' tales) much better for the animal as well. It's simple: spayed or neutered animals are better behaved and healthier. Females spayed before their first heat cycle are healthier than those that aren't. (Ask your vet, it's true!) Neutered male animals are better behaved and have fewer problems with aggression. Neutering reduces roaming and fighting and most animals lose the desire to constantly mark their territory. Animals that have been spayed or neutered also tend to live an average of two to three years longer than unsterilized pets.

Pets and Us

Many of us live a stressful existence. As you run from place to place with a cell phone glued to your ear, it can be a challenge to just stop for a minute and look at the world around you. Fortunately, those of us with pets have a live-in example of how to be "in the moment." Dogs and cats don't worry about deadlines and they don't nag you (except maybe for dinner). You may have noticed that a dog sleeping in the sunlight is rarely stressed out. Dogs can be endlessly amused simply by watching an ant crawl across the floor or by chewing on a toy.

Many studies have shown that owning a pet is good for you. Although a pet isn't a substitute for human companionship, people who have pets are less likely to become depressed. Having a pet forces you to think about something outside of yourself and your own little thoughts. Coming home to feed or let out the dog gives you a sense of purpose and responsibility. Someone is depending on you.

A recent study showed that owning a pet can actually have a beneficial effect on your blood pressure. Apparently those who had adopted a cat or dog had lower blood pressure readings in stressful situations than their pet-free counterparts. This study is one of many that indicate that owning a pet can keep us healthier and happier for longer.

When you have pets you are never alone. Even as I sit here typing away, four canines are quietly sleeping on the floor. It's only a matter of time before one of them leaps up and does something really dopey or makes a disgusting sound. Who can remain completely serious in the midst of all that silliness? If laughter is the best medicine, pets can be a great prescription for the blues.

Unfortunately, when this human–animal bond is broken, the results often affect far more than the pets in the family. In homes where spousal or child abuse exists, animal abuse often happens first. In fact, many women who would otherwise seek shelter end up staying with an abuser because of threats to kill the family pet.

Fortunately, the link between animal abuse and family violence is becoming more well known and publicized, so that in some communities law enforcement and animal services are working more closely. Most humans struggle and stress over problems of their own creation. Pets can be a valuable window into a simpler, more peaceful existence. Adopting a pet is a way to add more love into your life and that's certainly a good thing.

Is Adoption Right for You?

The purpose of this section is simple: to make sure you're really ready to take on that shelter dog or puppy. Millions of dogs end up homeless because their former owners didn't stop to think about the impact a dog would have on their daily lives. So even though you're excited about saving a shelter pooch, remember that once you bring her home, your life is going to change.

Some of these changes will be emotional, since many shelter dogs need extra love and patience. Others will be lifestyle changes. You'll need to make adjustments to your routine, your housekeeping, and your schedule. It's also important to consider the financial challenges of dog ownership. If you have children or other pets, you should consider the impact your newly adopted pet will have on their lives.

Before you actually start visiting animal shelters, spend some extra time with this section. Try to imagine what life with a dog will be like. This little adoption "reality check" will pay off in the long run for both you and your dog.

Time and Patience

When it comes to owning a dog, the two most important things you need to have are time and patience. You need time and patience for feeding your dog every day, housebreaking him, brushing him, cleaning up after him, walking him, taking him to the vet, playing with him, training him, and most importantly, for loving him. All this has to happen whether you feel like it or not.

Not everyone is temperamentally suited to dog ownership. People relinquish dogs to animal shelters for a lot of different stated reasons, but generally it comes down to a person's lack of time or patience to deal with the realities of dog ownership. So if you are considering getting a dog, first be honest with yourself. Many of us have complicated and busy lives; it's not a sin to have little time and less patience. On top of everything else going on in your life, can you deal with a dog loudly throwing up in your hallway? If not, maybe you should look for a more low-maintenance type of pet than a dog.

Should You Get a Dog?

After a bit of self-reflection, it's time to consider a few lifestyle realities. Before you let yourself fall in love with the first puppy you meet, you need to ask yourself a few questions. When you get a dog or puppy, you are changing your life for the next 10 to 15 years. Change can be stressful, so think about the ramifications of adding that furry face to your household.

1. Money. Getting a dog costs money. Your new pet needs food and other dog paraphernalia such as a leash, collar, and toys. Taking your dog to the veterinarian costs more money. It's unfair to the animal to deny him or her these basic needs. If you can't afford the cost of routine upkeep and veterinary care, don't get a dog.

2. Lifestyle. Honestly evaluate the environment you'd be bringing a dog into. Are you about to make any major life changes, such as having children, moving, marrying, or divorcing?

A Personal Quiz
- Do you travel a lot?

- Does your landlord permit pets?

- Are you away from home all day? (If so, are you willing to pay someone to take care of your dog while you are gone?)

- Do you have time to give a dog the attention it needs and train it?

- If you plan on getting a puppy, do you have the time and patience to deal with housebreaking? (You will have to clean up the inevitable accidents and take the puppy outside innumerable times.)

- Are you healthy?

- Are you allergic to pet hair?

- Do you demand a meticulously clean home?

Consider your answer to these questions. All of them are based on common reasons dogs are relinquished to animal shelters. In fact, many shelters have a pre-adoption form that is used to screen prospective adopters, so it's good to think about these issues before you head to your local shelter.

If you can't meet the animal's needs for any reason, save yourself and the dog a lot of heartache and don't adopt a dog. A pet is not something that should be considered disposable. Like adopting a child, adopting a dog should be for life.

Choosing a Breed

If you answered all the questions and still are committed to getting a dog, now it's time to think about what type of dog you want. Your new four-legged friend will be sharing your life for a long time, so it makes sense to do a little research on the various types of dogs. Different breeds have been bred for different purposes and learning a little bit about the history of the breed can help you avoid dogs with characteristics that are undesirable in your household.

Even if you are considering a mixed breed, you can make a better decision if you know something about the breeds that make up the mutt. Libraries and animal shelters have a number of books you can look through to learn more about dog breeds. If you have access to the Internet, numerous dog sites also have vast amounts of breed-specific information.

When you start researching dog breeds, the first consideration is size. If you live in an apartment, are elderly, or small, you probably should avoid giant or high-energy breeds. Your personality also comes into play. If you hate grooming, you should avoid longhaired and double-coated breeds, such as collies or huskies. Along the same lines, if you are compulsively neat, you may want to get a shorthaired breed that won't leave quite as many tufts of hair around your house. Active people may want an energetic breed that they can take jogging or hiking, such as border collies or retrievers. But if you don't exercise now, don't expect a dog to change you. If your idea of recreation is reading in your recliner, you may want to look at smaller and more sedate breeds such as corgis or basset hounds.

Your dog will be with you for years to come, so take the time to figure out what type of dog fits you and your lifestyle. Both you and your new friend will be better for it.

Breed Checklist

I want this type of dog:

Gender
Male ____   Female ____

Size
____ Small (1–30 pounds)

____ Medium (30–50 pounds)

____ Large (50–100 pounds)

____ Giant (101+ pounds)

Energy Level
____ High Energy

____ Moderate

____ Low Energy

Exercise Needs (per outing)
____ Significant (45 minutes to 1 hour)

____ Moderate (20–30 minute walk)

____ Light (Stroll around the back yard)

Fur
Long Hair ____   Short Hair ____

Personality - Exuberance
____ Extrovert (loves everybody)

____ Middle of the road (friendly)

____ Introvert (more aloof)

Personality - Dominance
____ Dominant

____ Medium

____ Submissive/Shy

Compatibility (Must like)
____ Children

____ Cats

____ Other dogs

____ Other_____

Smarts
____ Sharp as a Tack

____ Moderate

____ Slow and Steady

Make a copy of the checklist page and fill out the questionnaire. Take your answers with you when you meet dogs. People at animal shelters or in rescue want to help you find the dog that best matches your criteria. This quick checklist can help them help you!

Acquiring a Dog

Now that you've made your decision to adopt, the search begins!

When you decide you want a dog, these are your main options:

1. Get a dog from a pet store.
2. Get a dog from a responsible (show) breeder.
3. Get a "free" dog from an ad in the paper or that wanders onto your property.
4. Get a dog from a shelter or breed rescue.

Of course, this book is about adoption and rescue, so option number four is the one I hope you will choose. I also discuss a few issues surrounding option three, since many people end up owning "free" dogs this way.

Visiting animal shelters can be both fun and stressful. Depending on the shelter, you may suddenly find yourself confronted with dozens, even hundreds of potential doggie companions. You may experience powerful emotions, including confusion, indecision, and even a little anger. All those wonderful dogs you see there who need homes makes you wonder how people could be so heartless.

At times like this, remember that you're doing your part. By choosing to adopt a shelter dog, you really are making the world a little more humane and giving one special dog a great life. Remember that the nominal fee you pay to the shelter means more than you realize. Take the word of a former shelter volunteer: every adoption is a triumph for the folks who keep those shelter dogs healthy and find them good homes!

You can also reduce your stress level by being prepared. If you worked through the previous pages and did your homework, your task of choosing the right dog will be much easier. You'll have a good idea of the type of dog that will fit most comfortably into your living quarters and your family, which should help a lot when you're confronted with all those big soulful eyes and wagging tails!

That said, always listen to your gut feelings, and your heart, when choosing a shelter dog. Looks aren't everything, especially when it comes to canines. All loving, happy, healthy, well-socialized dogs are beautiful. If you don't have a good feeling about the shelter, the staff, or the animals, walk away. In literally every part of the country, and in even the most remote areas, there are always plenty of dogs up for adoption. You can even start your search online at sites like:

http://www.petfinder.com or

http://www.pets911.com

In this chapter, I cover all the adoption basics, including what to look for in a rescue group, the truth about "free" dogs, and what to do with that stray dog you'd like to make your own.

Ready? Let's go find your new canine friend!

Adopting from a Shelter

As the owner of two "North Idaho Special" dogs, I think mutts are great dogs. Even if you want a purebred, however, a shelter dog is still a bargain. My golden retriever Tika (a shelter alumna) is a purebred. In fact, approximately 25–40 percent of the animals that end up in U.S. shelters are purebreds. Shelter staff see AKC papers all the time. It's no big deal.

When you adopt a dog from an animal shelter, you often receive a package that contains food and coupons, a collar, an identification tag, a handbook explaining dog care, and a free health exam for your new pet at any local veterinarian. At the shelter, the dog receives a full set of shots and is wormed and temperament tested. If it turns out that the veterinarian finds a health problem that was missed at the shelter, you can return the dog, with no questions asked.

If you and the dog are incompatible for some reason, most shelters let you return the dog. Someone from the shelter also may call you to make sure you and your new dog are doing okay and to help with advice if you are having problems with issues such as housebreaking or unexpected behaviors.

Breed Rescue

Many people are under the impression that the only way to get a purebred dog is to go to a pet store or breeder. However, this is not true. As I said, approximately 25% of the dogs that come into shelters are purebreds (like my dog Tika). However, a shelter may or may not have the breed you want at the time you want to get a dog.

Although many animal shelters will put your name on a list and contact you when a particular breed of dog comes in, waiting for the right dog to arrive may take a while. Purebred rescue groups are another option. Dogs in shelters or whose owners can't keep them often get a second chance through a rescue group that is dedicated to saving a particular breed. (As I mentioned in the introduction, my dog Leto came from a rescue group.)

Over the years, rescues have been formed for virtually every type of purebred dog. They can be a wonderful source of healthy, well-mannered, spayed or neutered pets for your family. In some cases, the rescue may be just one person who loves and is knowledgeable about a particular breed. Other groups may be involved with national breed clubs or larger rescue networks. In any case, a reputable rescue can be a tremendous source of advice and information about a breed.

So now you've decided to save a life and adopt a dog through rescue. Finding a rescue club for your favorite breed is your next challenge. A good first step is to call your animal shelter. Because shelters tend to work with many rescues, they may be able to give you a contact number. If they don't have one, you also can try doing some research on the Internet. There are many sites dedicated to breed rescue and the American Kennel Club site (www.akc.org) lists the national rescue coordinators for each breed.

The Darker Side of "Rescue"

Although rescues may sound like a great option if you're looking for a particular breed of dog, you should know that not all "rescues" are legitimate. The darker side of rescue is that not all groups who claim to be "rescuing" animals out of shelters really are. Many so-called rescue groups are just fronts for puppy mills, backyard breeders, or worse. Instead of paying big money for purebred dogs, these "rescues" just pluck them out of shelters for a few bucks. Instead of saving animals, they are contributing to pet overpopulation by breeding even more animals to make some quick cash. In fact, sadly some shelters won't deal with rescues at all for this reason.

Legitimate rescues often have expert-level knowledge of the breed and can provide the veterinary care, training, socialization, screening, and information necessary to make successful placements. If you are thinking of getting a dog through rescue, ask a LOT of questions of the rescue group. They should give you complete and thorough answers.

If any animals on their premises aren't spayed or neutered, ask why. Look around the facility. If it looks (or smells) like a puppy mill, it probably is. As when visiting and evaluating a shelter, trust your instincts. Be very suspicious, and if you get a bad feeling from the person or their facility, find a different rescue.

Parking Lot Pups

There's a time and a place for everything. When you need food, you go to the grocery store. When you want to find a mean deal on household items, you head for a flea market. Neither of these places are good places to get your next dog, however.

It may seem innocuous enough to "adopt" that adorable puppy in the parking lot, but think about what you are doing. Grocers put the candy in the checkout aisle for the same reason people give away puppies in parking lots. They're hoping for an impulse purchase. However, getting a dog on a whim is often a big mistake. And it's why an estimated 50% of the animals you see being given away in parking lots and flea markets end up at animal shelters.

When you get a pet from someone in a parking lot, you have no idea what conditions that animal has been living in. The animal may be ill or housed in squalid conditions. It may be a puppy from a family pet, or it may really be a front for a puppy mill. Even if the person giving away animals says they've vaccinated the animal, you rarely, if ever, get any proof.

Realize that the person will be gone tomorrow, so if there's a problem, you have no recourse. Young puppies are very susceptible to disease and could be infected with such diseases as mange, parvovirus, bordetella, or distemper. When you take that cute little critter home, you expose your own animals to these contagious diseases as well.

Reputable rescues and shelters vaccinate all animals and keep their living quarters clean and disinfected. Free "parking lot pups" are not such a bargain when you consider vet bills. You'll have to take the pup to the veterinarian to get it vaccinated, at the very least. If the animal is already sick, you may have to spend a lot of money in medical care or even have it euthanized. (Unfortunately, vets see this type of scenario far too often.)

Talk to reputable rescues and shelters about their policies. If you have problems or concerns, you want to deal with a shelter or rescue that will be there tomorrow to help you.

Finder's Keepers

Another way people tend to acquire "free" dogs is by finding them. A lot of confusion surrounds the concept of pet ownership. People often deny ownership of pets that have been living on their property for years. Conversely, just because you find an animal, that does not make it yours.

The laws are reasonably clear: the "owner" of an animal is generally described as the person who owns, keeps, harbors, possesses, has custodial care of, or acts as caretaker. That means the stray dog you've been feeding for the last 6 months is yours. And as the owner, you may be held liable for any damages that animal causes to someone else's home or property.

The problem with pets is that unlike a lawn mower or other personal property, an animal can wander off. Don't assume that a pet you find has been "abandoned" or "dumped," even if you live out in the country. An owner may be frantically searching for the animal. It's your responsibility to report any animals you find to the local authorities or animal shelter.

If you report the animal and make an honest attempt to find the owner, but no one comes forward, generally, you become the owner by default if you keep the animal on your property. Check the local laws in your area, but before you adopt an animal in this way, make sure you understand your legal rights.

A Puppy for Christmas?

Almost every year, some advertising executive has a great idea to run a TV commercial that includes an adorable fat yellow puppy with a big red bow around his neck sitting under the Christmas tree. However, I'd like to suggest that you avoid the temptation to give a puppy for Christmas.

Most people are extremely busy over the holidays and unfortunately, the sad reality is that some of those Christmas puppies end up at shelters in January. Think long and hard before you decide to give anyone a pet as a gift. Be honest with yourself and consider your situation.

Is the nature of your job such that you have more or less time over the holidays? If you work in retail, for example, you may have a lot less time. But if you are a teacher, you might have some time off.

Any pet, but especially a baby like a puppy needs a lot of extra attention when you first bring it home. The new furry member of your household should be a priority—remember that he may be a member of your household for the next 15 years. It's also important for everybody to learn the home routine (especially for housebreaking purposes). It's not fair to the puppy if you won't be able to let him out or spend time with him during the chaotic holiday season.

Puppies need to be watched constantly. Ornaments, wires, lights, tinsel, and other holiday paraphernalia can be dangerous to a curious young pet. It's a lot easier to deal with a new pup after the decorations have been put away.

With all these caveats in mind, it's not always a terrible idea for people to get pets over the holidays. For example, those spending the holiday season alone may benefit from the company of a new furry friend. People without kids or who are retired with extra time available may do well sharing the season with a new dog.

However, you really should never give a dog to someone who is not expecting it. Getting a pet should be a family decision (even if your family is just you). Shelters are filled with furry gifts that were "returned." A dog is never a good surprise, since the recipient may not be able to take on the financial and personal responsibility for another living creature for the next 15 years. Not to mention the fact that choosing a dog is a very personal decision. It's not one that should be made for someone else.

If the latest adorable puppy commercial has tempted you to get a dog, talk about it with your family. Look at it as an educational opportunity. Wrap presents such as a collar, leash, and a book on pet care (like this one). Then visit an animal shelter or rescue after the holidays, so everyone can pick out the new family friend together.

Dog Personality Tests

As with people, you aren't going to like every dog you meet. Different dogs have different personalities. When you select a new canine companion it's a good idea to keep that fact in mind. As I mentioned earlier, if you are a couch potato, it's probably a good idea to get a dog that matches your sedentary habits. A high-energy or pushy dog may drive you insane.

With a puppy, it can be difficult to predict what he will be like when he grows up, but there are a few things you can do to try and make an educated guess. Some dog personality traits develop early, so you can get a glimmer of the dog your puppy will become.

Unfortunately, many people assume that if they get a particular breed of dog, the dog is destined to behave in a certain way. A given breed of dog is likely to behave in some ways because of genetic makeup, but stereotyping a breed of dog is foolish and has resulted in many a bad dog–owner match.

At my house for example, I have Tika, quite possibly the most high-energy golden retriever in North Idaho, and Leia, an extremely mellow border collie mix. If I were convinced that all golden retrievers are mellow and border collies are intense, I'd be doomed to disappointment.

Dogs are not something you just pick up off the shelf like a box of baking soda; they are individuals. A dog's genetics obviously play a role in his personality, but so does his experience. Dogs that are raised in a good environment have a better chance of developing into normal, happy, social dogs. The converse is unfortunately also true. Dogs raised in abusive or inhumane conditions are more likely to have problems.

Although some controversy exists as to how accurate personality or temperament tests are, you may be able to learn a few things about your puppy or dog before you bring him home. These tests generally measure a dog's confidence versus shyness, and dominance versus submissiveness.

The tests vary, but all of them involve careful observation of a dog's reactions to certain stimuli. For example, one test is to pick up a puppy and hold him under the front legs. Hold the pup out at arm's length for a few seconds. Puppies that struggle and kick their hind legs are considered more dominant than those that do not.

In another test, you roll the puppy onto his back and place him in the crook of your arm. You then put a hand on his tummy and look into his eyes. Dogs that don't struggle to get free are considered to be more deferential to humans than those who do.

You also can test fearfulness and skittishness by seeing the dog's reaction to an everyday sound. One approach is to drop a set of keys behind a dog that's walking away. If the dog completely freaks out, he may be easily frightened.

Beyond these basic "temperament" tests, you should find out whether or not your puppy can deal with other members of your household such as dogs, cats, or kids. Paying attention to the dog's reactions and body language is the key to learning about his personality and determining whether or not it's a match made in heaven.

Bringing Your Dog Home

As with people, part of a dog's emotional makeup is based on past experiences. Sometimes you adopt a dog that came from a wonderful home, but sometimes a dog has a "checkered past."

No matter what happened before, your adopted dog has no way of knowing what the rules are at your house. However, with a little understanding and TLC, you can help your newly adopted dog feel comfortable and become a part of the family.

The First Days

When you bring your new puppy or dog home, you should be prepared. If you spend some time in the pet section of your favorite store or start perusing pet catalogs, you'll quickly see that you could spend a small fortune on your new furry friend if you're not careful.

Essential Dog Supplies

Here's a list of the basics you need for your new dog:

1. Dog bowls. You need at least one bowl for water and one for food. Stainless steel bowls are easy to clean and don't get scratched easily. Scratches in plastic can harbor germs. Plus, some dogs have been known to chew their bowls. If your dog has a predisposition to play with his tableware, you also might want to consider a weighted bowl, so he doesn't throw food or water everywhere.

2. Food. Consult with your veterinarian on recommended food for your dog. Puppies, older dogs, and dogs with various health issues may require special foods.

3. A bed, crate, or both. If you are housebreaking a puppy, you may want to get a "sky kennel" to help with housebreaking. It also can be used as a carrier for trips to the vet and as a bed. Many dogs love having a special "den" to call their own. If your dog is older, you may want to consider getting a dog bed. Floors are hard on arthritic joints.

4. A leash. Contrary to popular belief, almost every area has a leash law, even in the "country." Keep your dog on a leash and keep the neighbors happy.

5. Toys. Your dog's age and chewing prowess determine the safest toys for him. Some dogs can decimate standard rawhide and plastic chewies in seconds. Hyper-enthusiastic chewing can result in blockages if the dog gulps down big chunks of a toy. In this case, look for heavy-duty toys like Kongs and Nylabones.

6. A collar and ID. A collar with identification is THE MOST important thing you can buy for your dog. I'll be blunt: not keeping identification on your dog is stupid and irresponsible. No good reason exists for your dog to be without a collar and ID, ever.

It's good to get your shopping done before you get the dog, but your dog will forgive you if everything isn't just "perfect" before you bring him home. Just be sure to get the ID on him ASAP. (After all, you just adopted a dog from a shelter; do you really want him to end up back there?)

More on Collars

A dog may be man's best friend, but a collar is your dog's best friend. For about $5, you can get a flat buckle collar that will last for years. Collars are more than just a canine fashion statement, they are important because of the accessories that can be attached to them. Identification tags are the most important item you can add to a collar. These inconspicuous inexpensive little pieces of metal save countless canine lives every day simply because the phone number on that tag enables someone to return your dog to you.

Even if you don't put on identification tags, write your phone number directly on the inside of the collar itself. Virtually everyone has a big black marker somewhere. Go get it and write your phone number in that collar. If people find a dog, they are likely to check the collar first. In fact, shelter employees generally remove every collar and check for any shred of identification. The collar itself is often helpful in identifying a dog. Patterned collars are often easy to remember and identify. However, the truly sad thing is that probably only 1 in 10 stray dogs that end up at a shelter are wearing collars at all.

A leash is another device you can attach to a dog collar. Not everyone you meet may think your dog is as wonderful as you do, and controlling your dog with a leash can help you prevent your dog from annoying other people in public. Controlling your dog has other benefits as well. Even well trained dogs will chase animals. It's very common for dogs playing off-leash to run off and disappear. The lucky ones end up at a shelter. The unlucky ones end up dead. No matter how well trained he is, you should not let your dog off-leash if there are moving vehicles nearby.

If you're on a budget, instead of buying your dog another chew toy, spend your money on something that can save your dog's life: a collar.

Dog Beds

Dogs spend about half of their day sleeping. Over the years, many people have asked me where their dog "should" sleep. They'll somewhat sheepishly ask if it's "okay" for the dog to be sleeping in their bed with them. I tend to think that there's no one right answer to that question. Some behaviorists do say that dominant dogs probably should not have the privilege of sharing your sleeping space. But if you have a well-adjusted dog who isn't trying to rule you with an iron paw, it probably doesn't make any difference where your hound snoozes.

The main thing is that you should be the one to decide. You should always be leader of your little household pack, so if you decide it's not okay for the dog to sleep on the bed, the dog never should. In our house, our dogs have never been allowed on the bed or other furniture. It doesn't seem to bother them. However, they do have their own beds in our bedroom where they retire. Each dog knows which bed is his or hers, and happily runs into it when we give the "go to your bed" command.

Most dogs like sleeping in your bedroom at night because you're in it. Dogs are pack animals and it makes them feel secure to be with the pack even when they're sleeping. If you're not home, they may prefer to retire to the bedroom just because the smell reminds them of you.

The type of dog bed a dog likes often depends on the dog. Dog beds can range from the simple to the very elaborate. If you're in the market for a dog bed, look for one that is durable and washable.

At our house, we have a number of types of dog beds, and a crate/sky kennel. In our bedroom, we have four dog beds we made. To keep the dog (and the hair) off the floor, my husband built wooden platforms out of plywood and 1x10 lumber. The bed frames look more or less like the ones you see in catalogs for $200. (Let's just say, we didn't spend that kind of money.) Inside the frame are baffled pillows that I made out of sheets and polyfill stuffing. For each one, I also made a cover like a giant pillowcase out of a sheet. Again, the cost was minimal, and I can throw the covers or even the entire bed in the washing machine when they get dirty.

We also have a couple of more conventional dog beds in our living room. We have a large round "bean bag" type bed with a removable cover. And we have a smaller one that is a foam nest shape with a washable cover.

Although many dogs actively will choose to sleep in dog beds, not all dogs prefer them. For unknown reasons, our golden retriever avoids all the dog beds in the living room. And Cami, the Samoyed mix, always prefers to sleep in her sky kennel. No other dog ever ventures in there.

The bottom line is that if you're trying to keep Rover off the furniture, investing in a dog bed might be a first step.

Bonding with Your Rescued Dog

The first few days with your new friend may be somewhat busy. Many times after you adopt a dog, the first thing you need to do is give Rover a bath. (If you suspect fleas or other infestations, a bath may be even more important.)

Combing and washing your dog is a good opportunity to start the bonding process. As you brush, be very careful and patient. Talk quietly to the dog and tell him how wonderful he is, but also spend some time feeling around and examining the skin and fur closely. Is it matted? Is the skin irritated? If you find lumps, inflammation, or other problems, take the dog to the vet for treatment.

Tending to the dog's physical health is important, but you also need to take his emotional needs into account. Give your dog time to adjust. Remember, everything and everyone in your house is going to be completely foreign to him.

If you have other dogs, don't trust the canines together alone for a while until everyone gets used to each other. You can use dog crates or baby gates to block off rooms while you aren't around to supervise.

Feed the dogs separately and don't let them share toys. Dogs can be extremely possessive about food or toys and "play fighting" can turn into real fighting quickly. (That's an extra vet bill you really don't want to have.)

Also realize that your dog has no loyalty to you yet and might try and run away. Be especially vigilant about keeping doors and gates closed. Always put the dog on a leash. Shelters are filled with "repeat offenders" that escaped from their new adoptive homes.

Be extremely careful with children and the new dog. Small children can do unexpected things and the new dog may not understand. Even a hug can seem threatening or frightening to a dog who is unaccustomed to it.

Give the dog a lot of time to settle in and adjust to all the new experiences in his environment. Don't try to force the dog to be your best friend immediately. The dog has probably been under a lot of stress and it's not fair to expect instant love.

Sometimes dogs bond really quickly, but other dogs take a while to be convinced you are worthy of their affection. But if you prove yourself a patient, predictable, and fair human, your new dog will come around.

Happy Spay Day

After you adopt a puppy, you may need to get it spayed or neutered. A lot of myths surround the subject of spaying and neutering pets, and probably the biggest myth is that getting an animal altered is bad for the animal. This is simply not true.

When a female dog is spayed, she can't get uterine or ovarian cancer and the possibility that she'll get breast cancer is greatly reduced. Another myth is that it's good to let a dog have one litter of puppies before getting her spayed. Medical research indicates the opposite: females that are spayed before their first heat cycle are typically healthier.

Some people also suggest that spaying makes dogs "fat and lazy." However, the only thing that will make your dog fat and lazy is if you feed her too much or don't give her enough exercise. Many people also think that spaying is expensive. But it doesn't have to be.

Many vets offer low-cost spay/neuter services and animal shelters often have cost-assistance programs as well. All you have to do is call. Spaying is a one-time cost that is minuscule when compared to the cost of providing care for a mother and a litter (or litters!) of puppies.

Plus, that "just one litter" contributes to the problem of pet overpopulation. Even if you find homes for the puppies, those puppies produce puppies and the problem grows exponentially and quickly. In six years, one female dog and her offspring can be the source of 67,000 puppies. There really aren't enough homes for them all. So, you should get your dog spayed not just because it's good for her, but also because it's the right thing to do.

Early Age Spay/Neuter

As I said, because of the health and behavior benefits, spaying or neutering is one of the most important things you can do for your dog. However, when you get a new puppy, that magic age of 6 months can really sneak up on you. Suddenly your formerly adorable puppy is acting a whole lot different as he or she starts sniffing around for a date. Then when you aren't looking, your canine teenager gets pregnant or starts running and annoying the neighborhood. Now you have big problems.

One way to avoid these situations is to get your puppy spayed or neutered earlier than the traditional 6 months. Getting an animal fixed at anywhere from 7 to 16 weeks of age is termed "early age spay/neuter." Although still sometimes considered "controversial" in the veterinary community, early age spay/neuter now has more than 10 years of research and published studies to recommend it. Although in the past there were concerns about the future health of the animal or the danger of the surgery, the research indicates that puppies and kittens suffer no medical or behavioral side effects. In fact, the American Veterinary Medical Association has endorsed early age spay/neuter. They say, "... AVMA supports the concept of early (8 to 16 weeks of age) ovariohysterectomies and gonadectomies in dogs and cats, in an effort to stem the overpopulation problem in these species." The procedure also is endorsed by The Humane Society of the United States, The American Kennel Club, The American Humane Association, Davis University School of Veterinary Medicine, Cornell University School of Veterinary Medicine, Pacific Coast SPCA, The Good Neighbor Animal Alliance Center, K9 Haven, Alley Cat Allies, and many more.

Veterinarians differ in their opinions of the benefits of early age spay/neuter, so ask. Many vets say that some of the problems they see can be prevented if the animal is altered before puberty.

As I pointed out, spaying a female dog before her first heat cycle has a number of health benefits. Plus, male dogs that come into vet clinics with fractures, gunshot wounds, prostate problems, and testicular cancer almost invariably haven't been neutered.

It's tragic that so many of these animals die unnecessarily from problems that could be prevented by spaying or neutering. If you think you "can't afford" to get your pet fixed, think about the long-term medical costs of not getting your dog fixed.

The Mythical Miracle

Lots of people don't get their purebred dogs "fixed" because they figure that breeding the dog is a good way to make a fast buck. Or maybe they want their kids to see the "miracle of birth." But before you think that you're going to make any money at it, talk to some breeders. When you find out what's really involved in breeding your dog, you may find spaying her is just a lot simpler.

Even the most conscientious and responsible breeders have problems. Nature is cruel and puppies die. The miracle of birth often turns into the tragedy of death. Even with careful planning, proper equipment, and the best care, puppies die. Seeing helpless pups die is an exhausting, expensive, and heartbreaking experience for everybody. Are you (or your kids) prepared to watch a puppy die or have a terminal puppy euthanized?

Even if you are lucky and all the puppies survive, the extra expense is considerable and you are unlikely to recoup the costs. First, the parent dogs must be examined for genetic diseases that occur in that particular breed. People purchasing puppies expect these certifications. For many breeds, you must have the hips x-rayed and certified as free from hip dysplasia. Other common tests include eye examinations by a veterinary ophthalmologist, blood tests, heart exams, and other tests for breed-specific diseases. Any of these problems can be passed to the puppies from the mother, father, or both.

Also realize that you will incur many extra food and veterinary costs. The mother dog and the puppies need to eat. Pregnant female dogs generally eat much more food than normal. You also will have to take the mother dog in for checkups and take the puppies in for examinations and shots. If whelping doesn't go well, you may also have to take the mother in for an emergency C-section, or witness your own dog's death along with the puppies.

When you look at the alternative, paying to have your female dog spayed starts to look like a good idea. Leave dog breeding to responsible breeders who know what they are doing.

Adjusting to the Family

Dogs are pack animals. They instinctively observe who does and doesn't "belong" in the pack, and what the pecking order is. In many cases, you won't have much information about your adopted canine's background, so when making family introductions you may be flying blind because you have no past experience to go on.

If your adopted dog is still a puppy, you have a golden opportunity to develop her family skills by exposing her to new experiences (a process called "socialization"). As far as your adopted dog is concerned, "family" isn't just you and your spouse, partner, children, and even elderly parents who live with you. It also includes all the other animals in your household, even cats! If people other than your immediate family enter your home regularly, such as a health care worker, household help, or dog walker, you need to make sure everyone understands their role in your dog's life (and vice versa).

To help make adjusting to the family easier for everyone, let's look at some of the most common scenarios you will face as you introduce your dog to her new "pack."

Canine and Feline Cohabitation

When I worked at an animal shelter, I was often asked whether or not a certain dog "gets along with cats." However, a better question is: "Can this dog be trained to get along with cats?" Most dogs will chase virtually any moving object. Carnivores have an instinctive behavior referred to as "prey drive." If something runs, the dog thinks, "must be prey" and chases. That includes cats. Your job as an owner is to tell the dog that this particular object should not be chased.

With the exception of a few dogs with a really strong prey drive, almost any dog can be trained to get along with the cats in your house. To get started, all you need is a leash and a baby gate or piece of wood to block off a doorway.

If your dog already knows basic commands such as "leave it" or "down" you may not even need a leash. If you see the dog chase the cat, tell him "no cat" and give him a "down" command. Praise him if he complies. If your dog doesn't comply, put a leash on him and let him drag it around, so the next time he goes after the cat you can step on the end of the leash and stop him. When he turns to look at you, give him the "no cat" and "down" commands. Reinforce the good behavior with lots of praise.

The baby gate is more for the cat than the dog. It lets you block off an area so the cat can get away from the dog to a safe place. Your cat will appreciate other dog-free areas such as a feeding place that's up high or away from nasty canine snouts. Some people put a kitty door into a closet so their cats can have a private area for litterbox and feeding times.

With a little bit of effort on your part acting as intermediary, it's easy to live a peaceful existence with both canines and felines.

Kids and Pets

When you get a dog, you need to step back and evaluate your kids' attitude toward animals. Many children have never had any guidelines as to the proper rules for dealing with animals. Some kids run up to animals recklessly and others shy away in fear when they encounter one. Learning respect for animals should be a big part of growing up, but the increasing number of dog bite incidents is clear evidence that parents aren't telling kids what they need to know.

Start teaching your kids about animals at an early age. Show them how to listen and learn about their animal compatriots by watching critters from a distance at first. Point out birds in the trees or dogs in the neighbor's yard and discuss the animal's behaviors. Visit zoos, shelters, ranches, and other places where animals are in a controlled setting. Show your kids how to approach animals in non-threatening ways and get animal-related books from the library to educate your kids on the roles animals play in our lives.

Teach your children to be gentle. You might show them how to stroke an animal gently on a stuffed animal first, then graduate to a friend's pet that you know is very gentle. Be sure to teach your child not to chase or hit any animal. Studies show that cruelty to animals is frequently linked to human violence and abuse. A kid that is taught to care about animals learns that animals *and* people are living things that should not be treated violently.

When you are researching getting a dog, have your child help you research breeds and read about pet care. When you go to look for your new dog, explain that owning an animal is a lifetime commitment and point out that animals should not be treated as disposable "throw away" toys. Also accept the fact that if your child is 10 now, and a dog lives to be 15, it may be just you and the dog in his senior years.

Show your kids the importance of having the pet as a family member, but don't expect small children to take full responsibility for caring for an animal. Getting a pet is a fantastic opportunity for education. Kids that have been taught to respect animals learn to look at the world around them in a more humane, caring way. And who wouldn't want that for their kids?

Retaining Pack Harmony

Living with multiple dogs is great if the dogs all get along. I've enjoyed the luxury of four-dog pack harmony for years now. But that's not always the case. When I was growing up, we had three dogs and one of them habitually tried to eat the other two. It was scary. I can report from personal experience that living with dogs that don't get along is a stressful nightmare.

Fortunately, behaviorists understand more about inter-dog aggression than they used to way back when. Basically, you and your dogs form a pack, and every dog knows where he stands in the pack hierarchy. Problems often arise when humans try to interfere with the pack order. In the canine world, there is no such thing as democracy or "fair." A pack has a dominant dog (alpha), second (beta), and so forth down to the last (omega) dog.

Generally, the dogs themselves determine pack order. The order generally hinges on personality, age, time in the pack, sex, and size. For example, even though our dog Leto is the newest member of our pack, he's still the dominant dog because he's a male and much larger than the next largest dog. Cami is the beta dog, because she's the most dominant of the three female dogs.

What many humans don't understand is that to retain pack harmony, you need to do two things. One is that you should be Ultra Alpha. Even the most dominant dog needs to respect you as the ultimate leader. Garnering respect isn't about literally dominating the dog in any mean or physical way. Instead, you always make the dog "work" for any desired result, such as sitting before being petted or fed. (I talk much more about the concept of leadership in the next section and throughout this book because it's extremely important in your relationship with your dog.)

In addition to being Ultra Alpha, you need to reinforce the pack hierarchy. If you coddle the omega dog, the alpha dog may view that as competition. With humans, there's a tendency to "root for the underdog" so they want to console the omega when things don't go her way. Ignoring the dominant dog in favor of the omega destabilizes the pack and can be the source of fights, as the alpha takes matters into his own hands (or paws).

When adding a new dog to your household, you should carefully consider how the new pack order will play out. Think about compatibility. If you have a very elderly shy dog, bringing home a boisterous, hyperactive dog is probably not a good idea. Always introduce the new dog to the old dog on neutral territory. Many times the dogs will immediately figure out that they like each other. Or not.

Even if the dogs seem to basically get along, be prepared for a few squabbles, especially in the initial phase until the hierarchy is completely settled. Don't interfere as they sort things out. Generally the pack order will restabilize. Again, supporting the "loser" can have a destabilizing effect. Feed the dominant dog first and pay special attention to him to reinforce the hierarchy.

If it seems like the problems can't be resolved, talk to your vet. Sometimes illness causes one dog to become a target. If the problem is serious, call in a professional behaviorist or be prepared to find a new home for one of the dogs.

Dog Group Names

Maybe it's just us, but we have a number of dog-related terms. In order of age, our dogs are as follows: Leia, the black border collie mix; Tika, the golden retriever; Cami, the white Samoyed mix; and Leto, the off-white Pyrenees/retriever/ whatever mix.

A long time ago, I read that you should only use the dog's name when you are talking TO them, not when you talk to other humans about them. So when James and I discuss our dogs, we call them, "the black dog," "the gold dog," "the white dog," and "the big dog," respectively. This terminology can get long-winded when you talk about multiple dogs.

So to explain the various pack dynamics in our life, we also have come up with collective hound terms. You call a group of cows a herd and a group of birds a flock, so eventually, we developed similar pack shorthand.

When we talk about Leia and Tika together, they are collectively, "the elderhunds." Leto and Cami together are "the white dogs." Tika and Leto are the "all retriever team." Leto and Leia are "the L dogs" or the "good dogs" (as they are the most obedient). Cami and Tika are the "jerk twins" (as the least obedient). And Cami and Leia are "James' dogs" because he likes them best.

It sounds complicated, but it's not. When I tell James, "the white dogs are snoring around my chair," he knows exactly which dogs I mean. And that's what communication is all about.

Understanding Your Dog

Once you have a dog, you are exposed to a different world. Dogs don't perceive things the way humans do and many people who end up having "problems" with their dogs, often simply haven't learned how to communicate in a way the dog can understand.

In this section I'll attempt to offer a few reasons why your dog does the things she does, or at least the best guesses of experts in dog behavior. "Guesses" is the operative word, because frankly we still don't know exactly why dogs behave in certain ways, or do certain things. Dogs clearly have reasons for what they do—all you have to do is live with a difficult dog who knows how to push your buttons to be convinced of that! But understanding what's going on in the dog's head can still be a challenge.

The point of this section isn't so much to analyze your dog. It's to help you develop a compassionate understanding so you can try to see things from your dog's perspective. Whether you're dealing with a serious and bewildering behavior problem like separation anxiety, or just a dog who's a bit cranky due to old age, understanding your dog can make all the difference.

Be Leader of Your Pack

As I mentioned earlier in the "Retaining Pack Harmony" section, whether you realize it or not, your dog views you and your family as his own private wolf pack. In the canine world every pack has its own dominance hierarchy. This pack mentality means that, in your dog's mind, you are either a leader or a follower. Understanding this one concept can dramatically improve the relationship you have with your dog.

As in the human world, leaders give commands and followers do what the leader says. Your dog's instinct is to figure out where he falls in the pack hierarchy. You may think you are your dog's "master" but your actions may be telling the dog something else. If you want your dog to follow your commands (instead of the other way around), you can do a few simple things to show that you are the boss. Being leader of the pack has nothing to do with harsh punishment. It has everything to do with consistency and setting limits.

You need to set the rules from the first moment you meet your dog. Because you are the leader, your dog shouldn't be calling the shots. For example, leaders control who gets fed when. You should get to eat your dinner first and you should make Rover "sit" before he gets access to his food bowl. The "sit" and "down" commands are powerful tools you can use to let your dog know you are the ruler of the roost. (I talk more about teaching these commands in the Educating Your Dog chapter.)

Before he gets to go out on a walk, make Rover sit while you attach his leash. If Rover is being a nuisance while you are cooking dinner, make him lie down and stay there. (I talk about how to teach your dog to do a "long down" in the training section.) If the dog gets up, put him back into the down position as many times as necessary until you (not the dog) decide it's okay for him to get up.

If Rover is lying in the middle of your way and won't move, don't walk around him. In a wolf den, dominant dogs lie where they want to and dogs lower on the dominance scale move out of the way. If you walk around your dog, your dog will assume this is an act of submission on your part. Also make sure you go through doorways before your dog. It sounds obvious, but pack leaders lead, so don't follow your dog. Even asking for affection can be an act of dominance from the canine perspective.

Dogs that demand attention are asserting dominance, so if your dog gets pushy, ignore him. When you are ready to pet him, ask him to sit first. In the leader-follower game, making a few little changes can have a powerful effect on the way you relate to your dog.

Dog Body Language

Although certain canine body language is specific to the dog, a few signals are more or less universal. Learning these mannerisms can give you an insight into your dog's mood and anticipate her responses. A few things are obvious. For example, a dog that is happy and excited will be wagging his tail, prancing around, and/or jumping around. A dog that is cowering in the corner is afraid. Here are a few other common canine mannerisms and their meanings:

Play Bow: Rear end up, front down, and tail wagging generally means, "I want to play."

Tail Wagging: Doesn't always mean that the dog is happy or friendly as is generally assumed. Some dogs also wag their tails when they are scared, agitated, or unsure about a situation. Look for other signals in addition to tail wagging to determine the dog's true mood.

Rolling Over: Generally means the dog is being submissive. In effect, the dog is saying, "You're the boss." Lots of times a contented dog also will roll over when she is happy and wants you to rub her tummy.

Tail Between Legs and Ears Back: The dog is afraid or feeling apprehensive about something.

Ears Perked Up: The dog is alert for some reason. During obedience class, the dog looking attentively at you with her ears perked up is ideal. It means your dog is paying attention to you and waiting for your next command (egad!).

Frontal Approach: A dog standing still facing another dog or person with direct eye contact, hackles raised, and ears and tail up indicates dominance or a sign of imminent attack.

Raised Paw: A dog who raises a paw with a bent foreleg is showing submission.

It can be interesting to just sit and watch a dog. By observing your dog, you'll see how her posture changes and how she uses her ears, eyes, eyebrows, lips, nose, mouth, tail, and coat to express her mood.

Dogs smell first, see second, and listen last. Often, they pay attention to your posture and mood more than your words. Your dog knows your body language, so if you take the time to learn her body language too, you'll be one step closer to improving the relationship you have with her.

LEIA

Mad Ears

Our dogs are all extremely good-natured creatures. But as in every family, little annoyances crop up. For example, our black dog, Leia, likes to sleep right next to my rolling office chair. This habit can be dangerous if I roll away from my desk. When I bump into her (which happens), she generally gets up in a huff with her ears pressed back alongside her head.

We call this ear configuration "Mad Ears."

Our dogs all have floppy ears, so when the dog is happy, the ears sort of hang down in a goofy kind of way. If the dog is alert, the ears are up and forward. But Mad Ears are a sign that the dog is somewhat miffed about something. Cami will get a case of Mad Ears when she feels it's time for dinner and I ignore her. She'll sit at the doorway of my office with her ears slammed back against her head and glare at me.

Fortunately, Mad Ears don't generally last long. Cami gets fed, Leia finds a new sleep spot, and order is restored to the canine universe. But for anyone who thinks that dogs don't have emotions or moods, I'm here to tell you that the ears say differently.

Canine Communication

Although you're never going to be able to have a debate on the meaning of life or the merits of dog chow with your dog, you can get a lot of information from your dog by closely watching her body language. In fact, once you figure out the signals, you can begin to predict what she'll do next. If you watch your dog, you can detect when she's feeling excitable, fearful, or aggressive, so you can anticipate and prepare for her actions before they occur.

Many dog signals are universal. As I mentioned, when a dog has her rear end up and front end down with her tail wagging in a "play bow" you can be pretty sure she is trying to invite someone (canine or human) to play. However, some signals depend on the dog. For example, right now my dog Cami is wandering around the hallway carrying a chew toy. She is making rrr-ing noises and has flattened ears and squinty eyes. If you didn't know her, you might think that the flattened ears and vocalizations mean that she is being aggressive or afraid. But nothing could be further from the truth. For Cami, these mannerisms signal that she is very proud of herself and wants everyone to know just how wonderful she is.

Even though tails, ears, and eyes can be a great indicator of canine mood, a lot depends on the breed. Some dogs carry their tails and ears higher than others. Cami is half Samoyed, so her tail normally curls over her back. If her tail is low, she's unhappy or afraid. But greyhounds or whippets naturally hold their tails this way, so unlike Cami, a greyhound with its tail between its legs may be perfectly happy.

Because of these differences, it can be very difficult to "read" a strange dog. This difficulty is why the staff at animal shelters or vet clinics take many safety precautions when working with the dogs they receive. It takes time and observation to learn a dog's body language and not doing so can result in serious injury. So be careful when you encounter a dog you don't know. Many dog bites are the result of a failure to communicate.

CAMI

The Mighty Woo

Cami, the fuzzy white dog, is notable not only for her blue eyes, but also for her prodigious "woo." Unlike our other dogs, Cami is able to sort of pucker up her face and make a resounding "woo woo" sound, when she's got something to say.

However, Cami only woos when she is suitably motivated. As a basically willful animal, she doesn't woo on command, or even reliably. No one particular thing can incite a woo. She has figured out that I think it's really cute though.

For a while, Cami would woo when she needed to go out. That woo was a useful woo. Since she has a small bladder, knowing when it's "outing time" can be key. During the course of the day, Cami also tends to woo around 3 pm. This woo may mean a) she's got to go out; b) she doesn't really *need* to go out, but she *wants* to run around and stomp the other dogs; c) she's bored and basically feels like being a nuisance.

Even though it's probably a futile exercise, I continue to try and figure out when Cami's vocalizations are meaningful. After all, it's really handy to have a dog tell you when she needs to go out. So I carefully look for signs that the woo might be different in some way. (Maybe this time the woo really means something!)

For example, 15 minutes ago Cami wooed. We went outside, stood in the rain, and stared at each other. Cami did nothing except sniff and stare. Clearly, I am going to have to accept the fact that sometimes woos have no meaning. They're just cute.

Walk the Dog

Although people pay a lot of lip service to the idea that exercise is important, the obesity statistics in the United States are a good indicator that most people don't exercise as much as they should. Even if you don't exercise yourself, it's extremely important for your dog's mental and physical health to get enough exercise.

There's an old saying that "a tired dog is a good dog." Many dog behavior problems are solved by regular exercise. Walking your dog every day is good for your dog's mental, emotional, and physical health (and it's not bad for you either). Be sure to cater your walks to the energy and fitness level of your hound. If you have a big dog who is bouncing off the walls, consider taking him for a longer walk or find a confined safe area where he can really run hard without the encumbrances of a slow-moving human (you). Conversely, if you have an elderly terrier who is content with a short spin around the neighborhood, don't sign him up for a 6-hour hike in the woods.

If you have a dog that likes to retrieve, it's even easier to give your dog enough exercise. You can remain a couch potato and let the dog do all the work. Most dogs are easily taught to retrieve and some dogs that are bred for retrieving often need almost no training. Even if you don't have a retriever per se, almost any dog will run after an object if you throw it. The tricky part is getting him to bring it back to you. But if you start at an early age and make retrieving a big game, the dog will get into the fun. Praise and reward the dog when he brings the object back to you. Eventually he'll figure out that the only way the game continues is if he returns the object to you.

Spending time with your dog is important to his mental and emotional well being, as well as his physical health. Dogs are pack animals and isolation goes against their basic instincts.

Even though a dog in a fenced yard is safe, too much time behind chain link can result in boredom and cause behavior problems such as excessive barking or compulsive licking.

Time you spend walking your dog offers an opportunity for you to bond, interact, and communicate with your dog. Even after a bad day when it feels like the world is against you, you can rest assured that when you take your dog for a walk, you'll be the greatest hero in his life.

Educating Your Dog

It's odd that people send their kids to school for years, yet seem surprised when their new dog doesn't psychically know everything about living life in your house. Sadly, dogs aren't omniscient and although they want to please, you need to take the time to educate Rover.

A recent study by The National Council on Pet Population Study and Policy (NCPPSP) discovered that 96% of the dogs surrendered to animal shelters had not received any obedience training. What this statistic boils down to is a lack of communication. Training doesn't mean classes or dog shows or tedious exercises. If people take 5 minutes to teach a puppy to sit, training happens, and communication occurs between the dog and owner.

When you get a new dog, one of the best things you can do is find an obedience class in your area and attend. Think of the time you spend at these classes as an investment. After all, you may be living with your dog for the next 15 years. If you can take a few hours out of your life to attend a standard six-week obedience class, it can reap rewards for as long as you own your dog.

This section has information on teaching your dog manners, standard training commands, and housebreaking. Since this book isn't about winning obedience trials, I focus on just the few simple commands you need to communicate with a family dog. Of course, more advanced obedience classes are available too. If you discover that you like training dogs, innumerable opportunities exist for you and your dog to enter competitions, or you might even end up with a new career helping other people train dogs.

Socializing Your Dog

Often you hear that you need to "socialize" your dog, but what exactly does that mean? The personality and behavior of an adult dog is affected by its genetics and its environment. The events (or lack of events) during a dog's puppyhood have a big impact on the dog your pup will become. You probably won't have any control over what happened to your new puppy during its first 7 or 8 weeks. But after you bring the puppy home, you can help her develop confidence by exposing her to new sights, sounds, and experiences. This process is called "socialization."

Basically, socialization is the process of introducing your new puppy or dog to new experiences in a positive way, so she doesn't end up fearful and upset about new experiences. As we all know, life happens. Happy, well-socialized dogs can adjust to new people and places without freaking out.

According to behaviorists, the most important socialization period for puppies is up until they are about 12 weeks old. This period is when much of their canine world view is formed. Your goal as puppy caretaker is to let your pup know that the world is okay and she shouldn't fear new things. Since the pup will be having a lot of new experiences, you want them to be as positive as possible. For example, if your pup's first trip to the veterinarian is traumatic for some reason, she may fear the vet's office for the rest of her life.

The first few weeks you spend with your new puppy are important in the socialization process. You are taking the little pup from everything she has known: her home, littermates, and her mom. So it's not unusual for the puppy to be confused.

Don't coddle your pup during this time, but don't overwhelm her either. Introduce your puppy to new experiences slowly in controlled situations. For example, introduce your puppy to a few new people or the neighbor's dog, but don't overwhelm her by having a huge party with 50 people and loud music.

To socialize your puppy, consider inviting people over to meet your new puppy. Introduce the dog to men, women, and kids. You also should let the puppy meet dogs, puppies, and cats (make sure any critters are vaccinated before they visit). Take your pup out with you to experience other places too. You might take him to parks or shopping centers, for example. Just make sure you are either carrying him, or he's on a leash. Taking him out and about also exposes him to the whole car experience as well. You should take him to the groomer or the vet, so he can learn about mundane things like having his toenails trimmed.

Show your puppy household items that either move or make weird noises like umbrellas or the vacuum cleaner. Encourage him to check out new items you bring into the house, like shipping boxes (which can be filled with exciting smells for the pup to investigate).

Also try rearranging random items, so the puppy gets used to change. You might fold a folding chair one day and leave it open another day. When it comes to introducing sounds, do it gradually. If you have a really loud vacuum cleaner, for example, run it in a room that's out of the way first.

The socialization process continues after puppyhood as well. Until the dog is a year old, it's important to make a conscious effort to expose the dog to new things. Take her out for walks, car trips, or even to work. Invite guests over and teach your dog how to greet people politely. Take her to obedience classes where she can learn how to be around dogs and people in a civilized manner.

As you go through the socialization process, there are two main things you don't want to do. First and foremost, don't scare or allow the puppy to be harmed in any way. Also, don't reward fearful behavior by cuddling, cooing, or coddling the puppy. Approach each new experience as you want the pup to do—confidently and happily. Often dogs look to their people for guidance. If you act like everything is fine, odds are good your puppy will too.

Dogs that aren't socialized during their first year often become shy and afraid of new experiences. So it's important to take the time to involve your new puppy in as many activities as you can. Having a well-socialized dog is better for the dog as well as the owner.

Nip Mouthing

If you have a puppy, in addition to socializing him, you need to teach him "mouth manners" because puppies, like human babies, have a natural urge to explore the world with their mouths. Although it's normal for puppies to use their mouths when they play with each other, it becomes a problem when this behavior carries over to their interactions with people. As the puppy gets older and his teeth get bigger, the same "play bite" that was cute now is painful and potentially dangerous. A little early training on your part can prevent big problems later, not to mention potential legal entanglements if your dog bites someone seriously.

When they are young, puppies learn "bite inhibition" from their mother and littermates. They learn how much pressure is too much from the reactions they get from the other dogs. Mom teaches her pup manners by yelping if he bites down too hard. As the owner of a new puppy, you must continue the lessons he began learning from Mom. You need to set boundaries, so your puppy knows what is and is not acceptable.

Puppies do need to chew, so be sure that your puppy has lots of acceptable chew toys, such as sturdy nylon bones. If your puppy starts chewing on you, however, make a hurt puppy noise to startle the pup and remove your hand slowly. You also may want to give a command such as "no bite" to help the pup associate his behavior with the correction. Most puppies want to please, so teaching even a persistent mouthy puppy is easy if you start early. Like everything else concerning dog training, consistency and patience pay off in the long run.

Preventing Dog Bites

The reason understanding bite inhibition is so important is because of the real safety issues surrounding dog bites.

In the United States, 50 percent of all children will be bitten by a dog before their 12th birthday. This dreadful statistic is behind a national effort to increase awareness about how to prevent dog bites. National Dog Bite Prevention week is in May and every year the Humane Society of the United States (HSUS) sponsors this event to help educate people about avoiding the problem.

Anyone who comes into contact with dogs must learn how to act properly to prevent bites. Parents need to explain to their kids how to deal with dogs. The majority of dog bites are from a dog a child knows, whether the family pet or a neighbor or friend's dog.

Dogs bite for three primary reasons: because they are defending their territory, afraid, or expressing dominance. Often it's a combination of all three, so it's important to pay attention to the actions of any unfamiliar dog. If he seems edgy or afraid, or is behaving oddly, he's more likely to bite.

It's especially important to learn and teach your kids a few common sense rules. If you encounter a tense, seemingly aggressive dog, don't approach it. If a strange dog comes up to you, stand still. Don't run and don't scream. Also don't look the dog straight in the eye. If the dog knocks you down, curl up into the fetal position and cover your face.

Here's a list of things you should tell your kids to do and NOT do when they encounter dogs:

Do NOT
- Stare into a dog's eyes.

- Tease dogs behind fences.

- Go near dogs that are chained.

- Touch loose dogs (i.e., any dog that is not on a leash).

- Run or scream when a dog approaches.

- Touch or play with a dog while it is eating or sleeping.

DO
- Tell an adult immediately if a loose dog is around or any dog that seems to be acting oddly.

- Stand still and be quiet if a dog approaches.

- Before touching a dog, ask the owner's permission.

- Before touching a dog, ask the dog's permission by letting it sniff a closed hand.

These little rules are simple, but clearly a lot of people don't know them. Every year, 650,000 bites occur that are severe enough to require medical attention.

Most dogs are friendly, so you don't need to walk around in fear of every canine you meet. But it pays to be cautious. You can love dogs, yet still care about people and your own safety too. With a little common sense and education, you can keep your pets, kids, and yourself free of injury and a whole lot of anguish.

Training

Many people seem to be under the impression that obedience dog training is somehow "unnatural"—something people make their dogs do to win points at dog shows. However, this attitude couldn't be further from the truth. We don't live in a natural world. When humans domesticated dogs thousands of years ago, we had to give Rover a few rules so that we could all peacefully cohabitate in the cave.

Learning Manners

Teaching your dog good manners is good for both you and your dog. When your dog knows proper etiquette, you'll enjoy her company more. So will your family and friends. Encounters with strangers, children, and other dogs won't be a problem. She'll be a reliable and enjoyable companion both at home and in public settings, and can go places with you, attend family gatherings, and participate in so many more aspects of your life. (Talk about a happy dog!)

Any friendship benefits from mutual respect. Most dog owners who have problems with their dogs have not earned their dog's respect. Respect doesn't come from domination or fear; it comes from good leadership. To be a good leader, you need to communicate with your dog.

The basis of good doggie manners is a healthy respect for your authority as "pack leader." Whole books have been written about pack dynamics, but it all boils down to you accepting responsibility. You take on the role of leader for your dog by being the dominant force in your dog's life. It's not about bullying your dog, but instead giving clear, consistent, and unemotional direction. Correct application of "pack principles" can actually prevent all kinds of problems, including dog bites.

Dog Training Tips

Most dog behavior problems can be prevented or solved if people put a little effort into dog training. Whether you learn from a class, a book, or a friend, training your dog is reasonably easy if you just look at it from the canine point of view.

Dog training would be a whole lot easier if dogs understood all the nuances of human speech, but they don't. Obedience commands work as a common reference that both you and your dog understand. After you've taught a dog to "sit," you both know what's supposed to happen when you give that command.

The key to training is consistency. Use consistent commands. Don't say "sit" one time and "sit down" another time. Rover will be confused. Be consistent with your rules as well. If Rover was allowed to nap on the sofa yesterday, it's unfair to expect him to understand that today when your finicky Aunt Martha is visiting, napping on the sofa is not okay.

Everyone in the family needs to agree on the commands to use and what is permissible and what is not. Then stick to it.

Another key to training is that it should be fun. If you tell Rover to "sit" and he does, you want to make Rover think that parking his rear end on the ground was the greatest thing he's ever done. Praise him lavishly and make a fool of yourself. Most dogs will think all this attention is pretty cool. Once Rover makes the connection that just sitting down makes you so happy, he'll be thrilled to do it again.

Dog Training Misconceptions

When it comes to dog training, it would be nice if there were a magic pill to suddenly "fix" all your dog's problems, but that's not going to happen. Although countless training methods exist, no one method works on every dog. Realistically, like people, dogs are individuals, so you may have to experiment a bit.

For example, if your dog isn't motivated by food, any type of training method that uses treat-based rewards isn't going to work very well. If you know what motivates your dog, it's a lot easier to encourage him to do what you want. Like that magic pill, a few other things you hear about dog training are definitely not true either.

1. You can't teach an old dog new tricks. This pervasive myth continues even though it's obviously not true. Even if your dog has slowed down physically, it doesn't mean he's suddenly not trainable. (When you turned 40 or 60, did you suddenly stop learning anything anymore?)

2. If I say it louder, he'll listen. When it comes to training, repeating commands and yelling are pointless. Repeating a command just teaches your dog not to listen to you. Say a command once and mean it. If the dog doesn't do what you ask, don't yell and scream. Your dog hears far better than you do. Instead, show him what you want. Correction and instruction is

not the same thing as punishment. You don't want your dog to fear you.

3. I already told him, so he KNOWS I don't like it. Dogs are not people. They pay attention to responses, and they live in the moment. They don't "know" what you are thinking from past experience. If they do something and it elicits a response (even what to you may be a negative response), they'll probably do it again. To many attention-starved dogs, being yelled at is better than being ignored.

4. I need to show him who's boss. Having a dog that fears you should not be your goal. Dogs respect leaders; they fear erratic, mean humans. You establish leadership by having the dog do things to gain a reward, such as sitting before receiving affection.

Again, dogs live in the moment, so punishing a dog for something he did hours ago just isn't going to compute. If you don't catch a dog in the act of doing something you don't like, you just need to pay closer attention next time.

Positive Reinforcement

The term "positive reinforcement" is used a lot in training. The idea is that your dog is motivated by a reward to do whatever it is you want it to do. I tend to think of it as the "what's in it for me" approach to training. If your dog has a worthwhile reason to do something, he will do it. If you can figure out what it is that motivates Rover, positive reinforcement can be a powerful way to shape or change behavior.

Timing is the key to using positive reinforcement in training. You have to give the dog the reward at the exact instant he's doing the right thing, or he can associate the wrong action with the reward. For example, if you tell your dog to "sit" and then he slumps into a "down" and you give him the treat, he'll think he's being rewarded for the "down." (Ooops!) Only reward the good behavior, not the bad. This caveat is why so many dogs continue to bark even after being told not to. For some dogs, any attention is better than no attention. When he barks, you yell. The dog views you yelling as a good thing, thus reinforcing the behavior. (Another oops.)

The tricky part in using positive reinforcement as a tool is that you must find out what motivates YOUR dog. For example, I have four dogs and they are motivated by different things. Cami is motivated by food. If I have a treat, she's the ultimate obedient model citizen; if I don't, she couldn't care less what I say. Tika is sensitive to touch. Petting her makes her extremely happy (sometimes too happy). Food didn't work well for motivation, especially when she was young because she couldn't focus long enough to eat. Leia is sensitive to tone of voice. A happy praising voice is a thrill for her, and she wags her tail almost every time. Leto is an affection junkie and likes food. Petting and praise are a big deal to him, but a little snack doesn't hurt either.

Some dogs are also motivated by play. Many drug dogs are trained with a short play session as a reward for finding something, and trained cats (yes, there is such a thing) like the ones in TV commercials are almost invariably trained using food.

All dogs are individuals. Experiment to find out what motivates your dog, and keep training sessions short and happy. Once your dog figures out what's in it for him, he'll be happy to do what you want.

The Power of Positive Reinforcement

When interacting with your dog, it's a good idea to think about your role in reinforcing behaviors. Many pets have their owners well trained. For example, suppose Rover scratches at the back door. You, as his dutiful human, then let him out. Ten minutes later, Rover scratches at the door to be let back inside. You, as the well-trained human, open the door, and Rover returns inside.

In this case, Rover's action is met with his desired response, so by opening the door you just "reinforced" the scratching behavior. Of course, letting Rover inside and outside about 79 times a day gets annoying, and now you have scratch marks all over the door too. But what many people fail to realize in this situation is that the human, not the dog, actually created the problem.

In training, any behavior that results in something pleasant is reinforced. Because Rover likes the human attention he gets going outside, and then coming back in, he's going to repeat the scratching behavior. Because he is rewarded every time he scratches at the door, he receives "continuous reinforcement."

Reinforcement has to happen at the time of the event or it won't be associated with the event. For example, if you tell your dog to sit, but then give him a treat after he stands up, what are you reinforcing? If the dog is standing, you just reinforced the stand, not the sit, which is what you were trying to reward. Just as with Rover at the door, when training, you have to reward the correct action every time (continuous reinforcement).

Along the same lines, if you decide you're not going to play doorman anymore for Rover, the key is to never again reward Rover by opening the door when he scratches. Again, consistency is the key. If you decide that you aren't going to reward the behavior anymore, you have to stop completely. Everyone else in the household needs to stop as well. If Rover is ever rewarded for scratching at the door, he'll keep doing it (this situation is known as intermittent or variable reinforcement).

The only way to extinguish a behavior is to never reinforce it again. As long as Rover thinks there might be some prayer of being let in, he's going to keep scratching at the door. Only when he realizes that his action doesn't work anymore will he stop. (Some dogs have long memories for this type of thing, so it can take a while.) Plus, if Rover subsequently finds a new way to get outside like chewing up the door, he just reinforced the behavior himself.

Intermittent reinforcement is a powerful thing, so extinguishing behaviors can be extremely difficult, especially if you can't get the whole family to buy into ignoring something they don't like, such as door scratching. It requires a tremendous amount of patience and often a lot of time. But if you're wondering why your dog does something that annoys you, consider the power of positive reinforcement. You probably rewarded that annoying habit at some point, so it's your own fault.

The Value of "No"

Dog owners are often kind, good-hearted people. Those who have adopted a dog from an animal shelter or rescue group often are even more so. Yet sometimes, this same kindness that causes people to take in a homeless dog can actually make their dog's behavior problems worse.

Although some positive dog-training methods seem to imply that you should never, ever correct your dog, I disagree. Like children, dogs live in your house. For everyone's sanity, anyone in your house should follow a basic set of rules. A canine that has run amok because no one ever taught him the meaning of the word "no" is going to turn into a spoiled brat as surely as any human would.

Dogs aren't dumb. They avoid bad experiences and gravitate toward good ones. Some kind-hearted people are so worried that their dog won't "like" them that they give into every possible doggie request. They allow the dog to jump up on them and essentially "boss them around" every day. For example, the dog might push his nose at the person, demanding affection. This seemingly innocuous activity can escalate into barking or even biting for attention. Or the owner overfeeds their dogs to an extreme because "they kept asking for more food." Unfortunately, nice people often have problems living with dogs until they learn the value of "no."

As I've mentioned, in your dog's world view, everyone in your household is part of his personal pack. Every pack has leaders (dominant animals) and followers (submissive animals) in it. This pack hierarchy can change over time as different dogs move up and down in the pecking order as their leadership is challenged. A dog can be dominant over one pack member and submissive toward another.

Just as a spoiled kid is always "testing" Mom and Dad to see what he can get away with, a dog is always testing to see if he can move up in the pack hierarchy.

These pack dynamics are at the root of many dog behaviors. When a dog is being bossy or pushy in some way, he is trying to express dominance over another pack member, including you. The "top dog" or alpha member of the pack in everyone's eyes should always be the human. Being alpha does not mean being cruel or harsh with your dog. However, like any good parent, you must be the one to set boundaries and ground rules. And that means saying "no" sometimes.

When your dog does something he shouldn't, correct him. However, you have to catch him in the act. Never correct a dog after the fact. If you missed it, too bad. Get over it and be more vigilant next time. If your dog is demanding something, make him work for it. This is where obedience training comes in.

If your dog wants affection, make him sit or lie down before you pet him. These seemingly small changes cause the balance of power to shift. Remember that if you want to be a leader, you have to behave like one.

Teach Your Dog to Sit

Teaching the sit command is absolutely the most important thing you can do to improve the relationship you have with your dog. It doesn't matter how old your dog is; he can learn to sit. And every time you give the command, you quietly, humanely, and positively establish your leadership over the dog. For this reason, many behavior problems can be helped or even solved if your dog knows the sit command. For example, here's an obvious one: your dog cannot jump if it is sitting down.

If you have a small puppy, teaching him to sit is easy, thanks to natural puppy curiosity. Keep your training sessions extremely short (5 minutes) and always keep it happy. Say your puppy's name and "sit" and hold your hand above the puppy's head. (If he's motivated by food, hold a treat in your hand.) When you say "sit," move your hand slightly behind the puppy's head. The puppy will raise its head to watch your hand and his rear end will lower. When the puppy's rear begins to go down, say, "good sit." Repeat 3 or 4 times or less if the pup loses interest. After a number of repetitions, the pup will start sitting without the hand signal.

Teaching an older dog to sit is almost as easy as teaching a puppy. The only difference is that the dog is larger and may need a little more encouragement to put his rear on the ground. The principle is the same however. If the head goes up, the rear goes down. Depending on your dog, the puppy technique may work. If he won't focus on you, leash your dog and get the dog's attention, so he is looking up at you. Say the dog's name and "sit" and pull up on the leash and push down on the rump with your other hand. If you are having trouble, you can try placing one hand on the back of his hind legs and the other hand on his chest. When you tell him to sit, press on the back of his legs so his knees bend inward. At the same time push back on his chest gently, so he folds into a sitting position.

Using any of these techniques, as the dog starts to sit, say, "good sit." Don't pet him until he sits all the way. Then pet him briefly and remain still for a few seconds. Then say "okay" or "free" to release him from the sit.

Teaching your dog when to stop sitting is almost as important as the sit itself. Gradually make the sits longer, try 20 seconds up to a minute until the dog really gets that sitting means "sit until I say it's okay not to anymore."

Taking those 5 minutes a day to teach your dog this one simple command can completely change your relationship with your dog and save you a lot of heartbreak and anguish in the long run.

TIKA

The Sit Stomp

Most dogs are experts at getting attention. In positive reinforcement training, you never are supposed to pay attention to a dog when he's doing anything bad, no matter how much you may want to yell at him. The theory is that behaviors that are ignored are "extinguished." Some attention-getting behaviors are quite subtle, however. Tika, who even on a good day excels at being bad, does have one rather cute socially acceptable way to get attention. We call it the "sit stomp."

Because Tika had so many behavior problems in her youth, we used the "learn to earn" behavior modification program extensively. It means she has to sit to "earn" anything she wants. For years, the words "Tika, sit!" were a constant in my life. She's much better now, and she still knows sitting is the way to get what you want.

Now Tika has turned sitting into her own little type of performance art. When she wants something, she comes over and sits behind my chair. Sometimes she's kind of quiet, so I don't notice her there. So she'll do the "sit stomp" which basically entails readjusting her rear end and forepaws repeatedly. In addition to the body rustling behind me, all this wiggling sometimes causes the tags on her collar to jingle too. The end result is that I turn around, which is exactly what she wants.

She usually does another sit stomp and wags furiously. So I tell her it's a very "good sit" and give her a pet. It's more proof that, even though you may think you are training your dog, in reality your dog may be training you.

Stay vs. Okay

When I was about 14, I took my first dog to an obedience class. My dog Rufus was extremely eager to please and did great in class. I learned how to tell Rufus to sit, down, and stay, but there was always a nagging problem in the back of my mind. After you tell a dog to sit, is he supposed to sit forever? At the class, it wasn't really clear when you use stay vs. sit. What duration counts as a stay? Shouldn't the dog always stay where he is when you say sit?

Even back then I thought it seemed like a bad idea for the dog to decide when to stop sitting, but I didn't know why or really what to do about it. Of course, Rufus was no dummy. He knew what sit meant and over time, the amount of time his rear was on the ground after he heard the command grew shorter and shorter. He figured half a nano-second was long enough to qualify as a perfectly good sit.

What I didn't know then is that as the leader of your canine pack, you should be the one deciding the answers to big questions like when the dog should stop sitting. Leaders make decisions; followers obey them. It may sound rigid from a human perspective, but dogs love knowing what to expect from their pack members. A fair and responsible leader is every dog's dream human.

Unfortunately, when I was 14, I wasn't a great owner, and outside of class, Rufus' behavior wasn't exactly award winning. At home, he was an extremely high-energy dog that was a gigantic pain to live with. Everyone in our family spent a lot of time saying, "sit." Rufus would sit for his nano-second and then we'd tell him to sit again. He had us figured out—make a complete nuisance of yourself and the humans will pay attention to you and say "sit" a lot.

By the time I got my next high-energy dog, I was smart enough to ask more questions. After attending one dreadful obedience class, where I was told I'd never be able to "do" anything with my dog, I found other trainers and did some learning on my own. (A word to the wise: if a dog trainer ever makes you feel terrible, find a new trainer.)

I learned that one way to remain in charge of canine situations is to use a "release word." Basically, in addition to using the standard obedience commands, you use a word as a cue for the dog to stop doing whatever command you said earlier. In our case, we opted for "okay" as our release word. (Some people use "free," which in retrospect is probably a better choice, since unfortunately, the word "okay" comes up a lot in conversation.)

In any case, at our house, if I say "Tika, sit," our dog Tika should sit until I say "okay." As you're teaching the command, you basically just extend the time that the dog sits before you use the release word.

Using a release word essentially eliminates the need for the command "stay," which as I suggested earlier can be sort of an abstract concept. After all, if you're wondering how long "stay" means, what do you think your dog gets out of it?

Teach Your Dog to Stay Down

Teaching your dog basic commands, such as sit and down are the first steps toward communicating with your dog effectively. When you teach any command, the key is to use the same word every single time to mean the same thing. Don't let the dog get away with only sometimes obeying a command. Like little kids, dogs constantly test your leadership to see if you really "mean" a command. Don't even utter a command if you aren't in a position to follow through with it. That just teaches your dog to ignore what you say.

As I mentioned earlier, teaching your dog to sit to gain a reward, such as dinner or affection is a great way to establish your leadership. Another leadership tactic is to have the dog lie down for an extended period of time until you say she can get up. This "long down" is extremely useful, especially when you are cooking or eating dinner when you want the dog out of the way. At our house, all four dogs have to lie down while we eat dinner, which makes for a much more relaxing meal.

We actually use two different "down" commands. When we say just "down," the dog has to lie down right where he is ASAP. This command is normally for short periods of time. In contrast, when we have the dog do a "long down" we generally use the "go lie down" command, which means essentially, "go find a spot you are happy with and lie down because you're going to be there for a while."

To teach the long down, the dog needs to know the "down" command to begin with.

To teach him how to lie down on command, first have him sit. Hold a small piece of food in front of his nose and say "down." As you say the command, also move the food down, so the dog's nose follows it. You may also need to gently press his shoulders to push him down into position. When he is down praise him lavishly.

If your dog isn't food motivated, you can try a different approach. Have your dog sit and then say "down." Grasp his two front paws and pull them forward as you push the back down. When he is down, praise him.

After your dog understands the command, to do a long down, tell the dog to lie down near you and set a timer for 10 minutes to start (eventually work up to 30 minutes). When the dog is down, praise her verbally, but don't let her leap back up. If she does get up, put her back in the down position. Stay nearby or even sit on the floor with the dog if you have to, if that's what it takes to keep her in the down position. Don't touch her, except to put her back into the down position. (You might want to watch TV or something to keep yourself amused.)

After the dog has been down for the amount of time you have decided, praise her and say, "okay" in a happy voice. "Okay" is the release word, which means, "You can do what you want now." (Some people use "free" instead of "okay" which again is helpful if you tend to say "okay" a lot in conversation.)

While the dog is in the extended down, she doesn't need to remain perfectly still. Dogs tend to wiggle around and switch flanks to get more comfortable. Crawling across the floor is not acceptable, however. (One of our dogs can crawl across a room in minutes.) The dog should remain in more or less the same spot.

As with any other training exercise, you should always attempt to be patient and fair with your dog. If the dog can't do 10 minutes, start with 5. Now that our dogs are older, they tend to fall asleep during a long down, proving that respecting the humans isn't really such a hardship after all.

Teach Your Dog to Come When Called

Few things compare to the sinking feeling you get as your dog runs the other way when you call him. Sometimes he'll pause for a moment to taunt you, then run the opposite direction even faster. Obviously, teaching your dog to come when called is an important command, not only for your dog's safety but also for the canine–human relationship. When you teach your dog the "come" command, you establish your authority over the dog and garner the dog's respect.

When you attempt to teach your dog to "come," always remember that the dog isn't stupid. No dog is going to willingly run to any human if the dog has had a bad experience once he got there. When training the dog, remember the old marketing axiom WIIFM, which stands for "what's in it for me?" Just as a buyer needs a good reason to part with his hard-earned money, your dog requires a good reason to respond to your command.

So with this in mind, your job is to make coming over to you the most wonderful thing that can happen to your dog. The "come" command should always mean that there will be a reward, whether a treat, praise, or a favorite toy. The worst thing you can do is to call a dog to you and punish it. If the dog has done something wrong, you must go over to the dog to reprimand it. If you don't take that extra effort, you will never have a dog that comes when you call.

The first goal in training is to get the dog's attention. When you give a command, precede it with the dog's name to get his attention. Start off with the dog on a short lead. Make him sit while you walk away. Turn around and say, "Fido, come" in a happy voice. With any luck, Fido will at least look at you. If nothing happens, pull the lead toward you to clue him into the meaning of "come." Once he arrives, praise him lavishly and maybe give him a treat if food is a big motivator for him. Always use the same command and never say it more than once. Practice is the key, and reliability will take a long time, so be patient. The reward is worth it.

Teach Your Dog to Walk on a Leash

Part of being a good member of the canine community is walking nicely on a leash. Even if you live on a 100-acre farm, you probably have leash laws where you live, so if you ever take your dog anywhere other than the back 40 (like to the vet, for example), your dog needs to learn how to walk on a leash.

Some dogs will just naturally follow you whether they are on or off a leash. Others need a little more convincing that where you are going is where he should go as well. For boisterous dogs that are over the age of about 6 months, you may need to switch to a choke chain for leash training lessons. A choke chain is a chain with large rings in the ends. You put the chain through a ring to make a loop that you slip over the dog's head.

Used correctly, a choke chain doesn't choke the dog. To give a correction, you just snap the leash quickly. This tightens the collar and then releases it, so the dog gets the hint, but you aren't literally choking him.

Most people have trouble with dogs that pull. As one trainer pointed out to me at a class a long time ago, the dog is attached to you, so you don't have to worry about what he's doing. Leaders lead. So pick up the leash and start confidently walking in one direction. Don't look at the dog; just go. The dog may run ahead. Don't say anything; simply change direction. The dog has to follow. If you do this repeatedly, the dog soon realizes he'd better pay attention to what you are up to.

If you are a small person and you have a large dog, you may want to experiment with other types of collars. For example, the "Gentle Leader" head halter is not really a collar at all. Unlike a regular collar or harness, a head halter controls your dog from its head, not its neck. These collars use the same principle as a horse halter: where the head goes, the body follows. After all, no one leads a horse around using a chain around its neck, so the obvious question is: Why do we do this with dogs? A loop goes over the nose and another loop goes under the chin and buckles at the back of the head. Although it looks somewhat like a muzzle, it's not. A dog wearing the Gentle Leader can open its mouth, pant, drink, and eat.

According to the Gentle Leader documentation, the halter works with the dog's instincts. The nose loop corrects in much the same way a wolf pack leader would grasp a subordinate wolf by the muzzle. And the pressure at the back of the neck from the second loop simulates how a mother dog handles her puppies. The result in many cases is a calmer, more focused dog.

Just as it takes a puppy a while to get used to a collar, it takes a while for a dog to get used to the loop over its nose. However, once the dog realizes that something good is going to happen when you bring out the halter ("oh boy, a walk!"), it can become a very positive thing.

Although my dogs have all been to obedience classes and know how to "heel," sometimes youthful enthusiasm would get the better of them. Certain stimuli, such as a wayward grouse, would compel Tika (my hyperkinetic golden retriever) to try and yank my arm off in pursuit. With Tika, the Gentle Leader was an incredible find. The transformation is nothing short of miraculous.

As astonishing as this may be to anyone who has met her, walking Tika is now a pleasure. Sporting her stylish green Gentle Leader, she calmly and quietly walks along next to me. If a troublesome grouse appears, a gentle pull on the halter is all it takes to return her focus to me.

On the other hand, unfortunately the Gentle Leader is not the be-all and end-all solution. As I said, dogs are individuals, and some dogs just can't seem to get used to the halter. My dog Cami is one of them. She hated the strap across her nose so much, she spent her entire walk trying to remove it. So it didn't seem worth it. The best solution for her is a "no-pull" harness that has straps that go under her front legs. It offers a bit more leverage than a choke chain. As a sled dog, she is designed to pull, and the harness makes it possible for someone small like me to keep her under control, even when she's seriously pulling.

Teaching your dog to walk on a leash takes a lot of practice. You need to take your dog out for daily excursions. Experiment with different collars and see what works. Walking together helps you bond with your dog and also helps establish your leadership, so it's a key element of dog training.

No, I Will Not Go

In life, we all encounter forks in the road. Choices must be made as to which direction one will take. Because Cami is a willful dog, she has to be leashed. So wherever I go she goes. Or wherever she goes I must go. Because she is a willful dog, she finds new and more creative ways to be stubborn while on a leash.

We live in a forest, so the opportunity for the dog and leash to get tangled up in trees is ever present, especially if you have a long retractable leash. Plus, Cami likes her privacy when she relieves herself, so she tends to go behind trees for her personal moments.

Unfortunately, running behind the nearest tree combined with a long leash often means going through 15 feet of tangled forest. The worst part is that, given the choice of returning to the trail by coming back out the way she came, or by going through a different part of tangled forest, Cami steadfastly refuses to go back out the way she came.

No amount of saying "no, Cami" and/or tugging on the leash will deter that animal from her stubborn need to tangle as much leash into the trees as possible. You can see the willful gleam in her eye as she realizes how long it's going to take us to extricate the leash from the branches.

One day, I actually caught her on one side of the tree and forcibly moved her to the other side. She was annoyed. But I have choices too. If there's one thing I've learned from living with that stubborn dog, someone has to be alpha and it had better be me.

Teach "Go to Your Bed"

One of the best commands I've ever taught my four dogs is "go to your bed." This command tells a hound to stop whatever he or she is doing, run off to the bedroom, and jump into his or her appointed bed. As I mentioned earlier, we have dog beds that we made that are essentially a wood bed frame with a washable pillow laid in it for canine snoozing comfort.

The "go to your bed" command is useful for a number of reasons. Most importantly, it establishes me as the pack leader. As I said, in the canine world, someone is going to be leader of the pack and everyone is a lot better off if that leader is you. Some experts claim that letting a dog sleep on the bed is not a good idea because the dog gets the idea he's at the top of the pack hierarchy. Others don't buy into that. I avoided the whole problem by making beds for the dogs. (As the one who washes the canines, I know when they had their last bath and how they smell, so I don't want them snoozing quite that close to me anyway.)

Another nifty element of the "go to your bed" command is that the dogs aren't allowed to leave their beds until we say so. If we have guests who aren't particularly fond of dogs, with the "go to your bed" command, we can get all four dogs out of the way with one quick, simple command.

From the dog's perspective, having a place that is definitely his or hers is important. As with humans, every dog should have a space where he won't be disturbed and can completely relax. Because our dogs each have their own beds and can't leave them once ensconced, there is no stressful canine jockeying for position to get the perceived "best" bed. This lack of conflict is good for everybody.

Although we have the wooden beds now, we taught some of the dogs about their place when we were housebreaking them. Because we used a crate for housebreaking, the original "bed" was the crate. (I talk more about crate training in the "Housebreaking" section.) Once the dog was reliable overnight, we swapped the dog bed into the spot where the crate was. Because each dog goes to a particular place in the bedroom, the association was already made.

An alternative to teaching the dog to go to a particular place in the house is to use a moveable bed and to teach the dog that "go to your bed" means to go to wherever the bed is located. Some people use a blanket that the dog knows is his "place." This approach is great for those who travel because you can put the blanket in a corner, say, "go to your bed," and the dog is settled in for the evening.

The key to training is to always make sure the bed is a safe place and associate it with good things whether it's a treat or a favorite toy. Avoid using the "go to your bed" command as punishment. If "go to your bed" is a good thing the dog will always eagerly and happily run off to his bed.

Housebreaking

Housebreaking can make or break your relationship with your dog. In fact, many dogs end up in animal shelters simply because their owners didn't bother to teach them proper bathroom habits. This section looks at the right and wrong way to housebreak a puppy, as well as what you should do when your housetrained dog suddenly has an "accident" in the house.

Also realize that when you adopt an adult dog, because of stress or prior experiences, he may have some problems in the housebreaking area. In this case, treat the adult dog as if he'd never been housebroken. In other words, don't assume he "should" know something. Maybe he doesn't. Just start over and be patient. If he was housebroken before, he'll pick up on the program again quickly.

The Basic Principles

When you adopt your new puppy, housebreaking is generally at the top of the "to do" list. Teaching little Rover or Roverette that your new carpet is not her personal toilet is job one. How quickly your new pup is housebroken depends a lot more on your behavior than on her learning ability.

The key is to know the times when a puppy has to "go." Puppies always need to go outside after they wake up in the morning or from a nap, after eating, after playtime, and before bedtime at night. Given the activities of the average puppy day, you can probably surmise that they need to go out a LOT. Although it may seem like you're endlessly taking your pup outside, a preventive approach is the most effective way to housebreak a puppy.

The other key to housebreaking is using a crate. When used correctly, a crate can make the whole housebreaking task go a lot more quickly. A dog has a natural instinct not to soil any area where it sleeps or eats. If your dog sleeps in a crate, this instinct for cleanliness will be an impetus for her to "hold it" until you can take her outside. For those who don't know, a crate is simply a cage or sky kennel that's large enough for the puppy to turn around, but not so large that she can relieve herself in one corner and go sleep in another.

Your job as owner is to get the dog outside when she needs to go. So when you see puppy finish her dinner, snap on a leash and take her outside. Always take her to the same area and use some command such as "hurry up" or "go potty." Once your puppy has done what she's there to do, praise her and take her inside. If she doesn't, take her inside and put her in her crate for a while, so you can keep an eye on her until you are ready to take her out again in about 20 minutes. Note that you should never use the crate as punishment and puppies should never spend more than a couple of hours in the crate at a time, except while sleeping at night.

Housebreaking Schedules

As I mentioned, housebreaking a puppy can involve a lot of trips outside because of a puppy's small bladder (after all, when you gotta go; you gotta go). Puppies are not physically capable of "holding it" reliably for any length of time until they are 6 months old. So, housebreaking can be difficult when you're at work 8 hours a day, 5 days a week. Although the process is a little more difficult than if you were at home to supervise all day, it's not impossible, and you can have a housebroken puppy and keep your job too.

The trick is to alter your schedule a bit so you can attend to puppy needs. First, get up a little earlier in the mornings so you have some extra time before you leave for work to take your puppy out twice: once right after you and the pup wake up in the morning and once after the puppy's breakfast.

Select an area of your home (preferably with linoleum floors) that can be blocked off, such as a bathroom or laundry room. Puppy proof the area and block it off with a baby gate. Place the puppy's crate, toys and a water bowl on one side of the room and some newspapers down on the floor at the back of the room. After her final morning outing, put the pup into her safe area during the day.

Until the puppy is 6 months old, either you or someone else will need to come at lunchtime and feed the puppy and take her outside afterward. If you can't take a lunch break, ask a family member, friend, or hire a puppy sitter. As soon as you get home from work, take out the puppy. Do it again after she eats dinner and once more right before you go to bed. After your puppy knows the routine, she'll do her best to "hold it" until you arrive to let her out.

Deal with Mistakes

No puppy (or human) is perfect, and during the housebreaking process, there WILL be "accidents." Count on it and accept it. If you can't deal with cleaning puppy excrement off your expensive Oriental carpet, think again about whether you're really ready to own a puppy. An adult (housebroken) dog might be more your speed.

In any case, assuming you can accept the fact that accidents will happen, what do you do about it? First, here's what you don't do. Do not ever, under any circumstance, hold the puppy's nose to the puddle or pile on the floor. Not only is it cruel, following that old wives' tale is counterproductive. Although the pup will recognize what the mess is, a dog is incapable of making the intuitive leap that you're angry because the mess is in the wrong place. Plus, punishing a dog "after the fact" doesn't ever work because studies show that if there is more than a three-second delay between the act and the punishment, the dog has no idea what it's being punished for, which results in nothing more than a dog that's afraid of you.

A better approach is to praise the puppy when she goes in the right place. If you do catch the pup in mid-accident, interrupt her. Startle her by making a loud noise such as clapping your hands. Then rush the puppy outside so you can praise her for going in the right place.

Cleaning Up "Accidents"

"Accidents" are a fact of life for dog owners. So is cleaning them up. However, the way you clean up the mess can have an effect on whether or not the animal uses that place for its "bathroom" again.

Experts say that you should never let your dog see you clean up the mess, so put the dog in a different room while you clean up. Dogs have a tendency to relieve themselves in the same spot over and over again.

Dogs have a vastly more sensitive sense of smell than you do. Even though you may think a spot is clean, your dog still knows that's where he left his "scent." If you don't completely clean the area, your retraining efforts will have no effect. As long as your dog can smell his scent, he will return to the same spot.

Because a dog's nose is so much more sensitive than ours, be sure to clean up with an enzymatic cleaner such as Nature's Miracle, which removes the odor to the dog as well. (Yes, after housebreaking three puppies, you know I've got a gallon-size jug of that stuff in my cabinet.)

The first step is to find all the soiled area. This involves using your nose and eyes. You may have to get up close and personal with your carpet to find old stains. You also can use a black light bulb to reveal old urine stains. Turn out all the lights in the room and use the black light to identify problem areas.

Next you must clean the areas so the odors are really gone. Remember, even if you can't smell traces of urine, your dog can. If an accident has just happened, soak up as much of the urine/

liquid as possible with a folded towel or a stack of paper towels. Stand or press on this pad until the area is barely damp. Now get an enzymatic cleaner such as Nature's Miracle and follow the instructions on the bottle. These cleaners actually neutralize the odor, as opposed to just covering them up. Avoid using cleaning chemicals such as ammonia or vinegar, since they don't eliminate the odor. Using other strong chemicals may also decrease the effectiveness of the enzymatic cleaner. Avoid using steam cleaners to remove urine because the heat can permanently set the stain.

After you have used the enzymatic cleaner, rinse the area with cool water. Remove the water by blotting again with a towel. By following these steps, you can begin the retraining process free of smells that distract your dog from doing the right thing.

Housebreaking a puppy may take a while, but look at the bright side: it's nowhere near as difficult or time-consuming as housebreaking a human.

More on Crate Training

Few things are as misunderstood in the dog world as the "crate." You hear people bandy about the words "crate training" as if it's something mystical. It's not. Done correctly, crate training can be useful in many situations. If you have a puppy, the crate can help with housetraining and keep him in a safe area when you aren't able to watch him. (Anyone who has ever owned a puppy can attest to the fact that you have to watch puppies constantly to keep them from damaging the house or themselves.)

When you go to purchase a crate you should get one that will fit the size of your dog when he is fully grown. It should be big enough so that the dog can stand up and turn around.

The concept of crate training revolves around the fact that many dogs like small, enclosed areas. They think of these cozy spots as a "den." If you train the dog to associate the crate with pleasant experiences, he will willingly go to his den whenever he wants a nap, to feel secure, or just get away from it all.

Be sure to place the crate in a high-traffic area, so the dog doesn't feel "banished" from the rest of the family pack. Try tossing treats into the crate to encourage your dog to go in. Another approach is to feed the dog in the crate. The bottom line is to get the dog to associate something good with going into the crate.

After the dog has been introduced to the crate, it's a good idea to get him used to being confined with the door shut. As I mentioned, we started teaching the command "go to your bed" to associate the crate as a sleeping spot.

The crate was in the bedroom, so we could listen for any urgent rustling or whining that might indicate a need to go out. (Housebreaking a puppy requires a lot of patience and a lot of late-night runs outside.)

Although the crate is a useful tool, you can't expect that you can leave the dog for hours and forget about her. Puppies need to go out a lot, and you shouldn't crate tiny puppies at all. Once the puppy is 9 or 10 weeks old, you can crate her for up to an hour. As the puppy grows, you can increase the duration. At about 4 months, the pup can be crated 3 or 4 hours. But even an adult dog should never be crated for more than 5 hours, except for overnight.

Some dogs are more amenable to crating than others. And some dogs can't deal with it at all. There are many stories about dogs that have literally eaten their way out of a crate. Dogs are individuals, so don't force the issue.

Our dog Cami was difficult to housebreak, so her crate was her bed in our bedroom for a long time. She finally did get the idea though, and now the crate lives in the downstairs hallway with its door open. The crate is still her preferred sleeping spot when she's downstairs. For her, going off to snooze in her "hut" is not a punishment; it's a pleasure. And that's how it should be.

Dealing with Behavior Problems

One of the ways dogs and humans are alike is that they're not perfect. Even the best-behaved dog can make mistakes or behave badly. When this happens, you have a responsibility to not just correct your dog, but to try to understand the cause of his behavior. Understanding behavior can be tough, since you can't have a heart-to-heart talk with Rover so he can explain why he's suddenly messing on the carpet.

To further complicate matters, with some adopted dogs, the unacceptable behaviors might be deeply ingrained from past experiences. They might even be the reason the dog ended up in a shelter in the first place. In this section, I guide you through some common (and not so common) canine behavior issues, along with tips that should help you understand what might be causing the problem.

Providing Structure for Insecure Dogs

Shelter dogs are often extremely insecure about their place in the family "pack." Dogs who have been adopted often have a lot of issues, so they require structure in their lives.

As I discussed in earlier chapters, the best way to provide that structure is to turn it around so that you, the dog's owner, are in charge. It's often referred to as the "learn to earn" or "nothing in life is free" program. Basically, the dog doesn't get to do anything unless you say so. These techniques are not just for dominant dogs; they help insecure and shy dogs build confidence as well. With any dog, it improves your communication with the dog and can avert many behavior issues before they start.

The main thing is to teach your dog to sit and then make him sit for everything. He has to sit before being allowed up on the sofa, sit before getting into the bed, sit before eating, sit before being petted, and so forth.

As with children, someone needs to be in charge. Dogs feel more secure when they have a set routine and a clear leader. That leader should be you. Many dogs that end up with behavioral or anxiety problems are extremely demanding when the owner is home. Whenever the dog demands food or attention, she gets it. So when the owner leaves, it wasn't the dog's idea and she becomes upset.

The answer is to provide a stable environment with clear ground rules. If you aren't the one in charge now, it's time to start exercising some leadership. For example, never let the dog "rush" the door ahead of you. Leaders always go first. They also decide when the dog can eat. Make the dog sit before she gets any food or attention. These small actions seem trivial, but they change your dog's relationship with you. Suddenly, the dog isn't directing the show anymore; you are. Without the stress of feeling like she needs to run the household, your dog can relax and maybe even take a nap.

When you leave the house, never make it a big production. Just go. It's an ordinary event for you and it should be for the dog. If your comings and goings have turned into a massive emotional situation, you need to tone it down. Make the dog sit before you greet her. If she won't sit, completely ignore her until she does. Again, you must be in charge.

Yes, it may sound somewhat boring to not let your dog get all excited, and make her sit all the time, but it speaks volumes to the dog. Little dogs in particular can be incredibly domineering, so it can be easy to cave and say, "oh you're so cute, never mind." Try to resist that urge! A 10-pound canine should not be in charge of your household.

Over time, as the dog gets better about knowing who is boss, you can sort of relax on the whole program a bit. My dogs are older now, but as soon as they start becoming pushy or snotty again, I re-institute the "sitting" program, so they regain a clue. Then everything is fine.

Of course, some problems are too complicated to tackle yourself. For example, if a dog's occasional growl turns into aggression and he actually threatens to bite, it's time to consult a behaviorist.

Sometimes Dog Problems are People Problems

Many "dog problems" stem from a lack of understanding. Many people approach pet ownership as something akin to owning a car: if it's broken, take it to be fixed. If it has too many problems, you return it to the dealer or sell it.

This "pets are disposable" attitude is why so many dogs end up in rescue groups and animal shelters. It's tragic because almost all problems can be solved with a little patience and understanding. A dog is a dog. It is not a small human, and expecting it to behave like one is unfair.

All pets in the household need to learn the rules, but the humans need a few rules too. We all have bad days and your pets will forgive you, but try to remember these simple rules for dealing with your pets:

1. Don't yell at your pets. They have better hearing than you do and probably hear your normal voice just fine. Yelling just scares them.

2. Don't try to train your dog when you are sick, angry, or incapacitated in some way. Inconsistent or erratic behavior doesn't make sense to your pet.

3. Always be consistent with your rules. If Rover is not allowed on the sofa, never let him on the sofa. He doesn't understand why today you are telling him to "get off the sofa" when yesterday you spent three hours curled up together watching TV.

4. When training, keep your sessions short and end on a positive note.

5. Above all, be patient.

Your dog loves you and the best thing you can do is love him in return. Like any family member, you learn to live with a few foibles because the companionship and love you receive is worth it.

Think About the Pets

Life is full of changes and if you don't think your dog notices, well, you're wrong. Many times behavior problems in pets can be traced to changes in their home life. After all, your dog lives there too. Major life events such as death, separation, or divorce cause a great deal of emotional distress and dogs pick up on it and become anxious. If people suddenly start shouting and arguing with one another, it has an effect on every creature in the house.

When it comes to your dog, your household and the people and pets in it are part of his pack. Members of the pack fighting or leaving will disturb the dog, which can result in behavior problems. Your dog doesn't understand what's going on in the human world and you can't explain it to him, so realize that your personal problems can be a source of canine behavior problems. According to behaviorists, when a couple separates, it's a good idea for the children and the dog(s) to stay together. Sharing a dog between two households rarely works well, since dogs are such creatures of habit. Continually interrupting and changing their routine frequently leads to problems, especially for older dogs.

Adding a new person into the household may cause problems for cats and dogs, especially if that person arrives with his or her own pets. It can take quite a while for everyone to adjust to the new arrangements and you should be on the lookout for jealousy.

If problems arise, feed the animals separately and don't leave prized toys on the floor that could be the source of a fight. Pets also may be jealous of human attention. If a cat hisses or a dog growls, don't correct them. Instead simply ignore the animal and walk away. The sound of a human voice could encourage more aggression, so teach the pets quickly that any display of aggression will just cause you to walk away and not "play" that game anymore.

The only thing you can be sure of in life is change. Take the time to try and understand your dog's reactions when life's changes happen.

Canine Teen Rebellion

Many people are surprised and dismayed to discover that dogs, like people, go through adolescence. And like human teenagers, canine teenagers get rebellious. When she is about 6–18 months old, your puppy will probably start testing her limits, and your patience. Even though your dog may look like an adult at this age, she is not done with her mental development by any means.

Canine adolescence can be a difficult time for everybody. In fact, most dogs that are brought to shelters because of "behavior problems" are brought in when they are between 8–18 months old. They've become "teen ogres" and their owners don't know how to handle it. The good news is that you can almost always solve these problems if you understand what is going on.

The first step is to get the dog spayed or neutered. Like every teenager, raging hormones are at the root of many problems. Second, give the dog lots of exercise. At this age, a dog's tolerance for boredom is at an all-time low. And if you don't give her something to do, rest assured she'll find something to do.

The third key to surviving canine adolescence is to only give the dog a command when you know you can back it up. If you tell your dog to be "down," and she gets back up, you have to go over to her and tell her to be "down" again. Yes, it's repetitive, yes, it's boring, and yes, it's necessary. Dogs are smart. If Roverette figures out that you only mean the "down" command sometimes, but not all the time, she learns that she only has to obey you sometimes. Like raising a human, raising a dog requires a tremendous amount of patience. But unlike human adolescence, canine adolescence only lasts a few months (and even better, they never ask for the keys to the car).

Jumping Dogs

Dogs that jump up on people are a nuisance at best and dangerous at worst. This problem is easy to correct and even easier to deal with while the dog is still young (and presumably smaller). Dogs that jump are generally doing it for one of two reasons: to greet you or to express dominance. Dogs that are excited to see you jump up to get closer to your face, so they can smell your breath, which is one way they use to identify you. Dogs that jump and remain still with their paws on you are vying for social dominance. If you push the dog away, these dogs become more frustrated, so they jump with even more determination.

You can use a number of methods to stop problem jumpers. One is to teach the dog to sit. Every time the dog approaches you, tell him to sit before he can jump up. Be sure to praise him enthusiastically when he does sit. If this approach doesn't work, you can enlist the help of a friend. Put a training collar on the dog and hold the end of the leash. Have your friend encourage the dog to jump by patting her chest and making happy, excited noises. If the dog jumps, pull him down and say "no" emphatically. Once he's on the floor, praise him. After a few repetitions, most dogs won't fall for the ploy anymore and will just sit down when you encourage them to jump.

Another approach you can use is based on the fact that dogs have an inborn reflex to withdraw their paws if you hold them. When the dog jumps, grab his front paws and hold them firmly until he tries to pull them away. As soon as you feel the dog move his paws, release them and praise him when all four feet are back on the floor. Alternatively, when the dog jumps, you can grab the front paws and walk the dog three steps backwards to throw him off balance. Most dogs are disturbed by this technique so that jumping quickly seems like a bad idea.

Many dogs that jump are brought to shelters because their owners "couldn't deal with it." This flaw doesn't have to be fatal, however. Depending on the size and temperament of the dog, one of these solutions coupled with a little patience can work wonders.

You Must Chill

When people come over to your house, you may find that not all of your guests seem to love your dog as much as you do. They may not appreciate the level of adoration your dog wants to convey as he runs around like a maniac, jumps, barks, and generally makes a complete nuisance of himself.

So what can you do to prevent this level of doggie mayhem? On the one hand, it's not fair to your dog to make him spend his days banished outside or locked in another room every time someone comes over to visit, but having him knocking over the table (or the guests) is unacceptable.

The first and most important thing you can do to help your dog gain some manners is to teach your dog to sit. As I mentioned, a dog that is sitting is a dog that is not jumping. Four on the floor is a good thing. Teaching a solid sit can be a challenge. The key is to do it often enough that the dog does it absolutely every time, even when he's excited. After you've taught the dog what sit means and he does it reliably in controlled situations, try turning it into a game. When the dog is really excited or running, tell him to sit. When he does, give him a treat and praise him like he's done the most fantastic thing ever. If you make it kind of like a kid's "freeze" game, the dog will start to think it's fun. Then keep doing it in increasingly challenging situations, such as around people he knows, then people he doesn't. The goal is a sit that happens every time.

Another good thing to do is remove the excitement surrounding homecoming. So when you or anyone comes through the door, the idea is to make the event as low key as possible. Do not say hello to the dog. Completely ignore him for 20 minutes. The dog will think you're weird and get bored. Only after he's calmed down can you go over, say "hi," and give him a treat for being such a good boy.

Then move up to trying this approach with other people as well. Tell your friends to completely ignore the dog until the dog chills out. I have to say that for this plan, it's often more difficult to train the people than the dog. My mother, for example, has a terrible time following this rule, but it does help.

Finally, if the dog is being a big pest for some reason, or begging at the table, it's helpful to have some commands that essentially mean, "go away." My dogs, for example, have three levels of commands. First is "go lie down." That means "yo dog, you may find a spot of your choosing and go settle your furry self there." If the dog is unable (or unwilling) to find a spot, the next command is just "down." That means, "get flat right now, at the exact spot you are standing."

Finally, for complete nuisance moments, it's handy to have a "go to your bed" command (see page 79). My dogs all have their own beds, so if I say, "go to your bed" all four will run into the bedroom and hop into their respective sleeping locations. They aren't allowed to leave until I say they can.

TIKA

Behavior: The Good, The Bad, and the Really Bad

After reading about jumping and spastic dogs, know that you are not the first person to have an out-of-control dog. The first two years of life with my dog Tika were less then idyllic.

Now Tika is a good dog. Given her background, upbringing, and temperament, she's pretty much the best dog she can be. Every family has an eccentric aunt or uncle in their family tree. You accept the idiosyncrasies and maybe roll your eyes and laugh. Tika is the good-natured goofball in our canine family.

But it wasn't always this way. Living with Tika for the first two years was a test of my dog owning endurance. When I got her, she had every behavior problem in the book. She piddled on the floor every time she got near anybody, she jumped on people, she chewed up the house, she chewed on herself, and was in constant motion all the time. I took her to two obedience classes where she was utterly mortifying. My classmates looked scared; the instructors looked sad. I continued to try every training method I could find information on.

Suffice it to say, the first 6 months were pretty rough. Most of the time I was angry, exhausted, and depressed.

Given all these behavior problems, many would have returned Tika to the shelter post-haste. But through it all, Tika was still my dog and she loved me. Passionately, vigorously, and completely hyperactively, but she loved me. I'm not an exceptional dog owner, but in Tika's eyes I was. So I vowed to make good on my commitment to her. It wasn't easy, it wasn't inexpensive, and it wasn't convenient.

Working with Tika required a lot of time, a lot of patience, and help from my veterinarian and a behaviorist. But it was worth it. Tika is now a dog we can live with and enjoy. Of course, Tika still isn't perfect and I'll never be able to do a lot of things with her just because she's a high-energy dog with a brain chemistry problem. But I can accept that.

And as Tika rests her big gold snout on my leg and looks up at me with her liquid brown eyes, I accept her too—lovable, silly goofball that she is.

Running Dogs

On a recent drive home, I saw not one, not two, but four dogs running on various back roads. Two were sitting along the side of the road, poised and ready to chase cars (fortunately, my vehicle wasn't interesting this time). I encountered another two dogs loping down the middle of the road straight toward me. It was still daytime and I drive pretty sedately, so I was able to see and avoid all of the canines with whom I was sharing the road.

This situation is not unusual, but it is unconscionable. Someone owns all these dogs and these people should not be letting their pets roam free. The tired old argument that, "we live in the country" is not an excuse to be irresponsible. Dogs roaming in the country are just as big a nuisance as they are in town. They pose risks to themselves and others. In addition to causing and being casualties of traffic accidents, roaming dogs are likely to contract and spread parasites and diseases such as rabies and distemper. Every day so-called "country" or "farm" dogs get shot. Dogs don't understand the concept of property boundaries, and in rural areas many people don't hesitate to shoot them.

Dogs are no longer wild animals. Just because they have fur does not mean that a dog can withstand prolonged exposure. Several thousand years ago, humans domesticated dogs, and now as pet owners it is our responsibility to take care of them. Dogs left to "fend for themselves" suffer and die, whether their former owners want to believe it or not. You don't get rid of your child just because it becomes inconvenient; the same should be true for your dog.

The obvious answer to all of these problems is to confine your dog. It won't get run over, shot, disease-ridden, or make a nuisance of itself. Do yourself and your neighbors a favor and install a fence before you get a dog.

Be a Good Neighbor

Part of being a pet owner is being considerate. You need to be considerate of your dog's needs, but also the needs of the people around you. Obviously, I love animals, but I don't want my neighbor's dogs in my yard. Here are a few of the arguments I've heard to try and justify inconsiderate dog ownership.

1. We live in the "country"/She's a "farm" dog.

A dog who roams the neighborhood, chases cars, bicycles, pedestrians, soils the neighbor's yard, or knocks over trash cans is a dog with an irresponsible owner, whether you live in town or in the country. Inconsiderate is inconsiderate no matter where you are. If your dog does not come when called EVERY time, you do not have control over that dog and it should be on a leash. And yes, contrary to popular belief, there is a leash law in almost all areas of the country.

2. It's too hard for me to walk my dog(s) on a leash.

Go to an obedience class and teach your dog to walk on a leash. Allowing your dog to roam at large is not only unsafe for the dog (since some people tend to shoot roaming dogs), but it also can cause legal problems. You can be liable for any damages, accidents, and bites caused by your dog.

I live on 40 acres of land. Two of my dogs always come when called. The other two don't. I know that. So anytime the two "problem children" are outside, they are on a leash. Being a responsible pet owner isn't very difficult, so be good to your dog, but also be good to your neighbors.

Dealing with Escape Artists

Animal shelters are filled with dogs that "got out." You might think that no fences exist anywhere. Any dog with sufficient motivation and insufficient confinement can escape.

Often people seem to think that dogs "jump" fences, but that's rarely the case. Usually, the dog has figured out how to climb out. I saw one dog that actually jumped up on a woodpile, climbed up on the roof of the house, and then jumped down onto a porch. The fence was perfectly intact and it took the owners a long time to figure out how the dog was getting out.

Dogs can sometimes use the fence itself to clamber up and over. I've seen video of an incredibly creative border collie climbing up and out of a chain link enclosure. There's a reason that border collies win agility competitions. They're agile.

Other dogs learn how to open a gate or systematically chew through a fence. Some dogs try combinations and spend a lot of mental energy determining their new exit route. If your dog is making such an effort to get out, you might want to figure out why your dog is so desperate to leave.

Dogs are pack animals and if they are spending hours and hours outside, they are probably bored and lonely. If that's the case, you should spend more time exercising your dog. Walking the dog is good for you and the dog. Or you could consider getting him a canine buddy.

Male dogs that haven't been neutered also will try desperately to escape because they are seeking female dogs. This sex drive remains undaunted until you get the dog neutered. If you have a female dog, get her spayed because an unneutered dog will find her eventually.

Another reason a dog may be eager to leave is because he's afraid of something. For example, if your dog is extremely afraid of loud noises and escapes every Wednesday right after the noisy garbage truck stops by, there's a big clue.

Once you have decreased the motivation for escape, you can attend to the reality of your fence. If you have a "climber," you can add an extension to the fence that tilts in toward the yard.

If you have a "digger," try burying chicken wire below ground level or lay chain link fence on the ground. You also can lay patio blocks or other large bricks that the dog can't dig up.

Whatever you do, don't punish the dog after you've found him. Dogs live in the moment, so punishing him for something he did hours ago is pointless and just confuses him.

Finding Your Dog

If the fence fails, then what? Every day gates are left open, fences fall apart, and dogs are lost. Losing a family pet can be traumatic, but there are steps you can take to help get your furry friend back home. Don't assume that your dog will figure out how to get home. Most dogs don't fare as well as Lassie. The odds of getting your dog back to you decrease the longer you "wait and see."

First make a few phone calls. Call:

1. The shelters in your area.

2. Your neighbors (or leave them a note).

3. The newspaper to place a free lost/found ad in their classified section.

4. Radio and television stations to ask them to make an announcement about your dog.

5. The city police or county sheriff (depending on where you live). Ask if they've found or impounded your animal.

6. City or county road department. Ask if they've had reports of an animal being hit by a car.

7. The local vets. Ask if they've treated any injured animals.

In each case, give the people you talk to a detailed description of your dog. Even if you don't know the breed, describing the color, length of hair, distinguishing markings, and what the tail and ears look like can be a big help in identifying your pet. Bring in a photograph if you have one. Also make sure you provide your name and phone number in case they see your dog later on. You also should put up posters (with a photograph if possible) in the area you lost your dog and on local bulletin boards.

After you get your dog home, take steps to make sure you don't lose him or her again. Be sure that he is always wearing a collar and identification tag. Also, if you haven't already done it, get your dog spayed or neutered. Remember, many pets that are wandering are following their raging hormones to the nearest potential mate.

Dealing with a Shy Dog

Like people, not all dogs are extroverts. Some dogs are worriers. New situations can be scary and make a nervous dog tremble and shake with fear. Some dogs are so anxious that seemingly normal household activities like vacuuming can be a seriously traumatic event.

If your dog cowers, hides, or trembles in fear, he is letting you know that he views whatever is happening as potentially dangerous, threatening, or painful. Dogs that have been abused or have experienced some other traumatic event often are extremely fearful. However, don't assume that every dog that cowers or trembles has been abused. My dog Cami has had the world's cushiest life and hasn't been abused. She is just shy; it's part of her personality and who she is.

If you have a shy dog who reacts fearfully to everyday situations, you can take a few steps to help him become more confident. Extreme fear can lead to desperate escape attempts, urination, or even fear biting, so helping Rover learn to cope is good for the entire family, not just Rover.

To increase your dog's confidence, you want to give him opportunities to be successful at remaining calm during situations he finds stressful. This technique is called desensitization and involves incrementally exposing your dog to the object or situation he fears. You increase the stimulation very gradually so the dog can slowly learn that, for example, the vacuum cleaner is not an evil entity that wants to kill him.

In this situation, you might leave the vacuum out in a low-traffic room for a few days. At first, the dog might avoid the room, but eventually he'll cross the threshold. When you see that, give him a treat. Since most dogs are curious, eventually, the dog may lean in and sniff the vacuum. At that point, give him another treat.

After he feels okay about that, try telling him to sit next to the vacuum and stay for 30 seconds. Then give him a treat. The goal is to reward calm behavior.

Eventually, you can work up to actually turning on the machine. You still want to go slowly however because you never want to have the dog become overly fearful during the desensitization process. If that happens, you often practically have to start over from the beginning. For example, the first time you could vacuum while the dog's outside. The dog may try and hide. But the next time you do it, he might not hide because he now knows the sound. After he's adjusted to that, later, you might try vacuuming while the dog is on another floor. Then the same floor, and so on, until you can vacuum without the dog caring about it at all.

Fear is stressful for dogs, and some dogs are so anxious that they can't focus enough to deal with any behavior modification or desensitization techniques. In these cases, veterinarians may suggest prescribing anti-anxiety medication to "take the edge off" so you can work with the dog more effectively. The drugs aren't a cure, but by decreasing the anxiety level, the dog can learn.

As noted, biting can be the result of extreme fear. If your dog becomes aggressive because he's extremely anxious and afraid, you need to get professional help from an experienced canine behaviorist. But for dogs that are just shy, a little patience on your part can help your dog develop the confidence he needs to lead a happy life.

Submissive Urination

Many dogs that urinate "inappropriately" don't have a housebreaking problem. Submissive or excitement urination is a common problem in dogs and is diagnosed based on the times it tends to happen. Submissive urination occurs when the dog feels threatened in some way. For example, if the dog urinates when you lean over her (a dominant posture) or when she's being scolded, it's likely she's letting you know she knows you're the boss. Dogs often lower their heads or roll over to indicate their submission. If you scold the dog, you only make the problem worse, since the dog is already "submitting" to your authority. The problem most often occurs in shy or sensitive dogs that are less than a year old.

Excitement urination is similar, but occurs at different times. This problem occurs during greetings or other times when the dog gets overly excited, such as during rough play. The difference is that the dog will not duck her head or roll over to indicate submission. Frequently, the dog will look sort of surprised to find he's urinating.

In either case, take the dog to the veterinarian to make sure that there is no medical reason for the urination. "Inappropriate elimination" is a sign of medical conditions such as diabetes, thyroid problems, hormone imbalances, urinary tract infections, and many other issues. If the dog is healthy, you need to work on the behavior. First, never scold the dog for the mistake; it will only make the problem worse! When you come home, keep greetings low key. Ignore the dog until he settles down. Don't approach the dog in a dominant way. Avoid direct eye contact and crouch down to the dog's level rather than leaning over him. Also, pet the dog under the chin rather than on top of the head. Try approaching the dog from the side instead of from the front. Teach the dog to sit and make her do so when you approach, so the dog has something to do other than roll and pee on the floor.

Remember that submissive and excitement urination is not a housetraining problem. Many times dogs "grow out" of submissive urination and with patience, you can change this behavior.

Barking Dogs

Barking is the way dogs communicate. Understanding why dogs bark is the first step to finding a solution for problem barking. Dogs bark for 3 primary reasons: 1. they are bored; 2. they are sounding an alarm that they've detected unidentified sounds, movements, or odors; 3. they are nervous or frightened (some dogs are extremely afraid of being left alone, a condition that is often referred to as "separation anxiety").

If the dog is barking because he's bored, you often can tell because the dog will sound bored. He will woof in a somewhat rhythmic and monotonous way. These dogs are generally ones that spend their days alone; they are barking to kill time. The solution is to make your dog's world more interesting. Spend more time with the dog and give him more exercise. If you know you'll be out for a while, give the dog entertaining toys such as a Kong filled with peanut butter. Tired dogs bark less and a dog can't bark while he's chewing (or sleeping).

If the dog is "alarm barking" the behavior was likely reinforced when he was a puppy. Scolding a dog or puppy for barking reinforces the behavior because the dog has gotten what he wanted: your attention. It may not be good attention, but to a lot of dogs any attention is better than none. Some dogs also seem to view people yelling at them for barking as just humans joining in the fun. Solving the problem usually involves distracting the dog and redirecting his behavior. For example, you might clap your hands then ask the dog to sit every time he barks.

If the dog is barking because of separation anxiety, you need to gradually teach him it's okay to be alone by leaving for short periods and praising him when he behaves upon your return. Separation anxiety can be a complex problem that manifests itself in many ways, so if you think that is the problem, you may want to talk to your veterinarian, a trainer, or behaviorist for more specific advice.

Digging Dogs

If you have found that your dog is embarking on his own personal excavation project in your yard, you've got a "digger" on your hands. Unfortunately, many dogs dig, and many dig for the sheer joy of it. As far as I can tell from observing my dogs, digging is just plain fun for certain canines. All of my dogs are diggers. Given their druthers, all my dogs would be thrilled to cover themselves nose to tail with mud, mud, mud every single day.

So if you don't want a yard that looks like a moonscape, what can you do? Your dog is probably digging for one of a number of reasons. He may be after something in the ground, such as a rodent. Or maybe he's hot or bored and trying to escape. With a little careful observation, you can probably figure out why the dog is digging and address the situation. If the dog is digging along a path and you have gopher holes, the problem is obvious. Deal with the gophers first, but do NOT use poison, which could harm your dog (talk to the folks at your local garden center or county extension office for information on safe pest removal).

Many dogs dig to create a cool spot. If the hole is in a shady area and the dog is lying in the hole, that's a clue. So, create a more acceptable cool area for the dog. For example, we got Cami, our Samoyed mix (who is ALWAYS hot), a $10 plastic "baby pool." On hot days, she lies in the pool contentedly splashing. If the dog is bored, he'll probably also be barking or otherwise expressing his displeasure. In this case, spend more time with the dog. Take him on walks, go to obedience classes, or play "fetch." Or get the dog a playmate and/or more engaging toys such as Kongs. Exhausted dogs don't dig; they sleep.

Dogs don't dig out of spite; it's a natural thing for them to do. If you have a dog that is just plain dedicated to digging, you can try providing a "doggie sand box." Choose an area of the yard where it's okay for your dog to dig and cover the area with loose soil or sand. If you catch your dog digging in a different place say, "no dig" and take the dog to his sand box. Praise the dog when he digs in the right place and make the unacceptable digging spots unattractive by placing sharp rocks, feces, or grass clippings into the holes.

A more expensive option is to provide a kennel area that has a slab or patio blocks as a floor, which is probably the ultimate solution to problem digging. In fact, patio blocks are the only reason my dogs' noses aren't completely covered with mud right now.

Marking

Dogs and cats live in a scent-oriented world that we can never completely understand. As territorial animals, they communicate "I was here" by marking their territory with urine. With their superior sense of smell, a dog can tell days later who or what has traveled through its territory. When Rover marks the local trees while out on his walk, nobody really cares or notices. But when Rover starts marking the walls or the sofa, the humans in the house tend to get quite upset. Unfortunately, many people confuse this type of marking behavior with a house-soiling problem. It's not. Dogs tend to mark vertical surfaces and frequently mark if they feel threatened.

Marking problems tend to happen most frequently in households where one or more animals are not spayed or neutered. Even if the dog doing the marking is neutered, the presence of an intact animal may compel the dog to mark territory. Dogs also often mark territory if they have conflicts with other animals in the home or even ones outside the home. For example, if a dog has conflicts with another dog he sees wandering through the yard, he may mark the house to prove it's "his."

The obvious first step to help with marking problems is to get all your pets spayed or neutered. Spaying or neutering may solve the problem completely. However, if the dog has been marking for a long time, you may also need to take steps to break the pattern. If you have conflicts among the people or animals in your home, you must find ways to resolve them to reduce the anxiety level. Sometimes this means giving up an animal, having new family members work with an animal, or consulting a behaviorist.

Also clean any soiled areas completely using an enzymatic cleaner such as Nature's Miracle. Try to make favorite marking spots inaccessible, or if that's impossible, change the area somehow, so it no longer seems like a prime marking spot. For example, one trick is to move the feeding area to a marking spot because animals won't soil an area where they eat. Remember that pets aren't people. A little understanding on your part can go a long way toward working through problems.

Fear of Loud Noises

In the spring, your dog may experience distress during thunderstorms. Some dogs are extremely affected by the barometric changes, flashes of light, and noise of storms. Most of the problems arise from destructive behavior as the dog tries to "get away" to someplace safe.

To deal with the problem, the first thing you should do is determine where the dog is trying to go. Many dogs rip out screens and tear up doors in their efforts to get inside. If so, consider installing a doggie door. If the dog is inside but really wants to hide under the bed, leave the bedroom door open. Remember, you are trying to figure out what the **DOG** thinks is safe, which may have nothing to do with what **you** view as safe. Do not punish the dog for her fear and do not lock her in a crate if that's not where she wants to be. (Note that some dogs do view their crate as their "safe" place, so if she wants to go in, let her, but leave the door open.)

Some dogs will respond to distractions. If the dog starts exhibiting anxious behavior, try distracting her with a favorite activity, such as a game of fetch. Give the dog lots of praise and treats to keep her attention. If she starts losing focus and behaving fearfully, stop what you are doing. When she's fearful, do not coddle or attempt to reassure your dog. These things will only make the problem worse by reinforcing the behavior. Act as if nothing is wrong. Your dog may think the sky is falling, but your job is to dissuade her by making it seem like everything is completely normal and totally boring.

If your dog is afraid of storms, the best thing you can do may be nothing. Dogs pick up on our emotions, so if you act like something terrible is happening, a dog that has a tendency to be afraid will figure you're on to something. Similarly, you should not cuddle or try to console the dog when he's afraid. You then essentially reward him for his fear.

When a storm arrives, act like nothing is going on. Be happy, laugh, and go about your normal routines. If your dog retreats under the bed, or to another place he feels safe, don't worry about him. The storm will pass and he'll come back out.

If the dog has developed serious noise phobias or anxiety, you may want to consult a behaviorist, veterinarian, or both. Certain behavior modification techniques may help the dog deal with the problem, but they must be used carefully so as not to make the problem worse. Various medications are available that can help calm your dog's fear. For milder cases, some people also have good luck with herbal, homeopathic, or other alternative treatments, so you can ask your vet about those options as well.

Thunder Paws

At our house, it's easy to tell when a thunderstorm is approaching because Leto, the large hairy white dog, starts panting.

At our house, 1 in 4 dogs has issues with thunderstorms. Leto gets very upset; the other canines just look at him like he's nuts.

Leto starts looking distressed long before the first clap of thunder, but his storm phobia isn't severe. He looks upset, pants, and tries to stay as close to me as possible. (Okay, you could make the argument that he stays close to me all the time, but during storms he definitely is distressed.)

However, some dogs go way beyond a little distress. During storms, some terrified canines react by going into a panic and may destroy your house in the process. Dogs have been known to eat furniture, break windows, and tear apart sky kennels in their effort to get away.

Experts don't seem to agree on which aspect of storms frightens phobic dogs: the flashes of light, the noise of thunder, or even the barometric pressure or electromagnetic changes that accompany a storm. Some studies have suggested that certain breeds of dog and rescued dogs may be more likely to have storm phobias. Leto was rescued from a shelter in Los Angeles and was extremely malnourished when I got him, so it is possible that he had scary things happen before I knew him. (Let's face it: parts of LA are definitely scary.)

Destructive Chewing

Obviously, all puppies chew, but sometimes chewing can go too far. When the dog chews on a doggie chew toy, it's fine. When he eats the sofa, it's a problem

For example, our first dog, Leia, was a model puppy, except for one thing. She didn't like being left alone. Like any determined youngster, she decided she'd better leave and find out where we went. Unfortunately, her approach was to chew her way out. We kept her in our basement hallway and she ate part of a post, some carpet on the stairs, and quite a bit of a homemade door that blocked off the upstairs. I patched the carpet, put wood putty on the post, and my husband put metal cladding on the door.

All of these things are now a distant memory, but I remember how upset I was when I found my downstairs hallway destroyed. Fortunately, we figured out what Leia's problem was and took steps to deal with it.

A dog may chew for various reasons. As I said, chewing in and of itself is not the problem. It's actually a symptom of something else that's going on. The key is to figure out what that something else is and deal with the underlying situation. For example, in Leia's case, it was obvious she was upset about being left alone, a behavioral issue that is often termed "separation anxiety."

Separation anxiety is a far different thing than just puppy chewing. All puppies chew; it's part of how they explore their world. Much like human babies, a pup wants to put everything in his mouth. So, your first job is to "puppy proof" your house to remove anything that could hurt him, like electrical cords and small ingestible items. The next step is to get a baby gate, so you can block off safe areas for your pup to hang out in when you can't keep an eagle eye on him. You also want to get your puppy a LOT of approved safe chew toys. A teething puppy is going to chew, so you want to direct that activity to the right place. A dog crate or sky kennel is another good investment, since you can use it as a dog bed at night to avoid any late night chewing sprees.

You should also realize that many adult dogs also like to chew, so you may be buying chew toys for a long time. If your dog is an "aggressive chewer," make sure you get sturdy toys like Kongs or Nylabones that Rover can't immediately destroy. You don't want to end up at the vet for a chew toy-related obstruction.

Anxiety-related chewing is unrelated to regular chewing. As with Leia, the dog is upset about something whether it's you leaving, thunder, fireworks or other loud noises, or stressful situations. The dog then chews at doors or windows to try and get out. Or she attacks items that smell like you, such as clothes or the sofa because the smell is comforting.

If your dog has anxiety-related chewing problems, talk to your vet. He may prescribe anti-anxiety medications along with behavior modification techniques to help your dog feel less stressed. In our case, the problem never got that bad because we got Leia a dog. We always call Tika "Leia's dog" because as soon as we got her, Leia was fine. In her case, all she needed was a buddy to make her feel less anxious.

Dog Aggression

Many dog owners don't think much about aggression in dogs. Healthy, well-adjusted dogs don't bite, growl, or snap at people or other animals. But not all dogs are healthy and well adjusted, and 4.3 million people are bitten by dogs in the United States every year.

The old saying that there are no bad dogs, only bad owners is not entirely true. Dogs are aggressive for a number of different reasons. Different types of canine aggression exist, and not all of them can or should be dealt with by pet owners.

Brain chemistry is a complex thing, and just as some people (like axe murderers) should not be wandering around free in society, so it is with dogs. Some dogs should never, ever be bred, sold, given away, or adopted out of shelters or rescues. If you go to a shelter or humane society and see a dog lunging, growling, and snarling at the gate, do not adopt it. Tell the shelter staff about it. Some dogs can't deal with being in a cage for long periods of time and go "cage crazy" as it's called in the humane community. These dogs should not be adopted and actually can pose a liability risk to the shelter itself.

Extended confinement is just one reason a formerly normal dog may start to exhibit aggressive tendencies. Others are abuse, pain, and extreme fear. However, some aggressive dogs behave that way not because of bad experiences or lack of socialization, but because of genetics.

For example, most terriers exhibit a very strong "prey drive" because they were bred to chase things. It's what they are designed to do. However, an overdeveloped prey drive can become dangerous if the dog starts stalking the kids and biting them, or killing the neighborhood cats.

If you are worried about your dog's behavior, your first stop should be the veterinarian's office. If the dog is biting because he is in pain, the vet can help. Thyroid conditions also can cause odd behavior, including aggression. At a minimum, the vet can spay or neuter the dog, which is a good idea since hormones trigger some types of aggression. If there's no medical reason for the dog's behavior, the vet also can refer you to a canine behaviorist.

You can help the behaviorist evaluate your dog by paying attention to details about the aggressive behavior. When does it happen and what does the dog do in response? Videotaping the dog also can be helpful. Behaviorists generally recommend behavior modification techniques to help mitigate or avoid problematic situations, but in most cases you have to remain vigilant. For example, if your dog has ever been aggressive around kids, you want to be very sure that the dog is never left alone with them.

If your dog is unpredictable, you need to get help immediately. Do not dump the problem on someone else by giving the dog away or taking it to a shelter. Safety for your fellow humans should always be your most important consideration.

What to Do About Dogs that Eat Non-Edible Things (Pica)

The official term for eating non-food items is pica. Pica isn't limited to rocks either, it includes habitually eating things other than food, such as shoes, carpet, wood, string, grass, or any other weird thing your dog might discover he likes. Unfortunately, pica can be a somewhat dangerous habit. Chewing rocks or other hard objects can break teeth or cause choking or intestinal blockages. As Cami has proven repeatedly, pica can cause vomiting and diarrhea as well.

Pica can be caused by either a medical or behavioral problem. Various digestive disorders may be related to pica, such as difficulty swallowing, or problems related to intestinal absorption. Other problems such as diabetes or a nutrient deficiency may be related as well. If your dog starts eating things he shouldn't, first you should talk to your veterinarian to rule out these medical problems. The veterinarian may want to run blood tests and urinalysis to check for underlying disease and organ function.

Once medical causes have been eliminated, it's time to consider the behavioral reasons for pica. Some dogs are so bored or anxious that they need something to do. Some dogs also will chew on things to get your attention. In fact, scolding your dog may actually reinforce the behavior. If the dog is looking for attention, you give it to him by scolding him. To an attention-starved canine, bad attention is better than no attention.

If the problem is behavioral, you have two main approaches. First, give the dog plenty of attention and exercise. A dog can't chew on weird stuff if he's asleep, so take him for long walks twice a day. You also can redirect the behavior by encouraging the dog to chew on "approved" chew toys. With retrievers and other dogs that like to "play ball" you can combine the two ideas and exhaust the dog by playing a lot of games of fetch.

The second approach is to just make sure the dog can't get at the problem objects. For example, if your dog eats rocks, take steps to make them unavailable. You also will need to keep her on a leash and make sure you don't leave her unsupervised in any area where she can get into anything she shouldn't. Yes it's more work, but your dog's health is worth it.

Canine Murphy's Law

Canine Murphy's Law dictates that the dog with the most sensitive digestion will also be the dog with the least discriminating palate.

Our dog Cami is a living example of this law. We refer to her as the Barfer Bear because if she eats anything that is not dog food, you can pretty much expect to see an unpleasant revisit of it on the floor later.

Of course, Cami's favorite hobby is wandering around the house or yard with her nose to the ground looking for something to eat. Note that I did not say she's looking for something "edible." Many things that Cami eats are not things that should be eaten. She favors rocks, dirt, hair, and even toenail trimmings.

Much like a human 2-year-old, if Cami can stick something in her mouth, she will. Relatively early in her life, I had to have her x-rayed after it was suspected that she ate a few of the rocks in her kennel. (Figuring that landscape materials cost less than more sets of x-rays, shortly thereafter, we purchased patio blocks for the kennel floor.)

In addition, because of her toenail obsession, cutting Cami's toenails is an adventure. It's a race to get at the little toenail trimmings you cut off before she does. If you've ever cut a dog's toenails, you know that the trimmings can travel great distances.

Usually I sit on the floor with her lying down. After every trim, I end up holding Cami's paw as she attempts to jet out of my reach after that elusive toenail. Cami is very focused and has a remarkable ability to crawl across the floor very quickly. So at some point both of us end up somewhat sprawled across the floor. It's a mess.

Thank goodness she's only got 18 nails.

Licking Dogs

When you have pets, the word "why" goes through your mind a lot. As in "why does my dog do [fill in the blank with something really disgusting]?"

So I've often wondered why my dog Leia takes every opportunity to lick any human who gets near her. What is she thinking? Is she tasting me? Kissing me? What is it? In every other way, Leia is a model canine citizen, but any time she can get away with it, she goes for a little slurp when people pet her. She knows we don't like it, so most of the time, she limits her slurps to guests who aren't ready to dodge her snakelike tongue.

Some dogs don't stop at licking hands. They will liberally bathe feet, faces, or legs. The theory is that to a dog, licking is a submissive thing. When the dog licks you, he is saying something along the lines of "you're the leader of my pack." Some dogs also lick as a substitute for mouthing. If a puppy has been trained not to bite or use his teeth on people, he may try licking instead.

Since we have more than one dog, I've noticed that the dogs sometimes lick each other, not just the humans in the house. Sometimes one dog licks the lips of another. Apparently, this licking signals deference to the other dog. In essence, the licking dog is saying, "I think you're great, and I know you're higher than I am in the pack hierarchy."

Interestingly, not just submissive dogs lick. For some dogs, licking becomes an attention-getting thing, which is a hallmark of dominant dog behavior. The dog basically knows he can get away with licking and doing it will get a rise out of you. In this situation, the best thing is to teach your dog to "sit" and then make him do sit any time he does something dominant. Pushy dogs test their humans constantly, so it's best to let the dog know who really is leader of the pack. (Remember, it is supposed to be you, by the way.)

In general, licking is a natural thing for a dog to do. A mother dog will lick her puppies to help the pups breathe, and to stimulate their digestion. Licking bonds the puppies to Mom and apparently helps their mental development as well.

Dogs also lick to groom themselves. After your dog has a bath or goes out in the rain, you'll probably find him busily slurping away trying to clean himself up. Unfortunately, with a dog, too much licking can turn into basically the same thing as obsessive-compulsive disorder in humans. A stressed dog may lick himself so much that he causes a sore. The sore is irritating, so the dog keeps licking it and a destructive cycle begins that is extremely difficult to break. In some cases, veterinarians will recommend a combination of behavior modification techniques and medication to help relieve the stress, so the sore can heal.

If you don't like your dog licking you, don't reward the behavior. A dog will continue to do things that seem to make their humans happy. If you smile and laugh while telling the dog, "no lick," the dog is going to keep doing it. Dogs are remarkably sensitive and pay attention to your body language and tone of voice as much, if not more, than to what you actually say.

Keeping Your Dog Healthy

. . . .

Keeping your adopted dog healthy is a lot like keeping yourself healthy. It all starts with regular hygiene, grooming, exercise, and tooth care, plus regular checkups at the doctor's office and preventative medicine like vaccinations. It also means administering medication when your dog is ill, and even researching all your options, like nutritional supplements or holistic medicine.

Even the most healthy, low-maintenance, ultra-fit mutt needs an annual health check and basic preventative medicine. If you've chosen an older dog as a companion, you'll need to be extra vigilant about her health. And all dogs need to be protected against the health problems caused by fleas, ticks, and other external "nasties!"

But first, let's start with the source of all doggie health, no matter what the age or background of your pooch: good grooming.

Grooming

Imagine how you'd feel if you never brushed your hair. Dogs have a lot more hair than you do, so no matter what the breed, every dog requires some sort of regular grooming. Over time, dogs that are never groomed can develop mats that pull on the skin and cause extremely painful irritation. This kind of neglect is lamentable not only because of the effect it has on the dog, but because grooming can be an extremely enjoyable experience for the dog and you.

If you get a puppy, you should introduce her to the grooming process as early as possible. Even though your pup may not have much hair yet, getting her used to the process can be helpful later in life when her full coat grows in. Make grooming a happy process, but start small. Puppies have a very short attention span, so begin by stroking her gently and quietly handling her paws, ears, and mouth area. Over time you want to work up to being able to touch all her pads and toenails, look in her ears, and open her mouth and touch her teeth. Praise the pup when she stays calm and quiet. If she loses interest, don't push it. Give the dog a toy and go do something else, so the session ends on a happy note.

You always want the puppy to associate grooming with something good. After the pup is used to being touched and handled, introduce the brush. Speak to her in a soothing voice and tell her how wonderful she is as you brush her back. For many puppies, the feel of the brush tugging her fur is a new sensation, so go slowly.

You can use the same technique with adult dogs as well. It may take a little time if a dog has never been brushed before, but with lots of patience and praise, the grooming process can be fun for everyone involved.

Dealing with Mats

If you've owned a dog for any length of time, you've probably discovered that things get stuck in their fur. For example, in late summer, after their run through the forest, my dogs are covered with small green "stickies" from native plants called pathfinders.

Depending on the plant, removing burrs and other prickly things is a relatively simple process. However, it's important to take the time to brush these items out of your dog's fur because when ignored, they can cause problems. Dogs that have been left outdoors often need to be shaved because their fur is so matted up with plant parts, they can no longer be removed.

Sometimes dogs don't need to get something in their fur for the hair to evolve into a mat. One of my dogs, for example, has silky hair behind her ears, which periodically tangles to the point that it turns into a mat. If this happens, you should remove the mat because eventually the fur can start to pull at the skin and cause irritation.

When you encounter a mat, first try to separate the fur with your fingers. If you have coat detangler or conditioner, you can spray it on the mat to help loosen the fur. Hold the mat and use a slicker brush to try and gently brush out the mat. Be careful not to tug at the mat. Next use a comb to try and work out the last of the tangles. Alternate between the slicker brush and comb until all the tangles have been removed.

If the mat is not located in a very noticeable area, or you can't remove the mat completely, you also can use scissors or clippers to cut out the mat. Be extremely careful because it's easy to accidentally cut the dog. Many mats are so close to the dog's skin, it's almost impossible to isolate the mat from the dog. (That's why they are painful to the dog...imagine how you'd feel if your hair were tugging you constantly.)

If you don't feel confident you can remove the mat safely, either use the brush/comb approach or take the dog to the groomer and let a pro handle it.

Washing Your Dog

There comes a time in every dog's life when you can't escape the inevitable conclusion: he smells. In fact, he smells really bad. When you know the dog is entering the room before you see his furry body amble through the doorway, action must be taken. Yes, Rover, it's bath time!

As doggie caretaker, keeping your canine clean is your responsibility. Unfortunately, you may dread bath time almost as much as Rover does. The good news is that not all dogs need to be bathed particularly often. In fact, bathing a dog too often can be bad for his skin because it strips off the protective oils. The frequency of bathing depends a lot on your dog. Some dogs just get stinky faster. For example, retrievers and other water dogs generally have oily coats (to repel water), so they get a case of doggie odor more quickly than some other breeds. Shorthaired dogs and dogs that spend a lot of time inside also generally need fewer baths than longhaired breeds or dogs that love to go outside and roll in disgusting things. Your nose will tell you how often you need to bathe your dog.

Before you wash your dog, brush him. Removing all the loose hair and mats makes the bath easier on everyone. Obviously, you have to wash less hair, but also on a longhaired dog, you are less likely to have matting problems if the dog has been thoroughly brushed out first. Water tends to turn small tangles into mats and small mats into big mats. If your dog has twigs, straw, or other pieces of crud in his fur, remove them. Clip out anything sticky like pitch or tar using clippers.

Once you have decided that yes, today is THE day, you need to get your bathing supplies together. Get everything you need in the bathroom before you go find Rover. The most important thing you need is dog shampoo. Dogs' skin is a different pH than people's, so it's not a good idea to use human shampoo on a dog.

You'll also need a lot of old towels. The bigger and hairier your dog, the more towels you need. Ideally, it helps to have a hand sprayer and a bathtub tether to hold Rover in place.

Once you have Rover in the bathroom, close the door. After you have him in the bathtub or shower, begin by thoroughly wetting down his fur. Follow the instructions on the bottle of shampoo, especially if you are doing a flea bath. Generally it's easiest to work in the shampoo if you water it down in your hand first. When you are done soaping up the dog, move to the rinse cycle. Rinsing is extremely important and generally takes at least twice as long as the soaping up process (that's why a hand sprayer is very helpful). You don't want any soap residue left because it can irritate your dog's skin.

When the bath is done, the dog will inevitably shake. Probably all over you. If you can, it's nice to have the dog do one really big shake while he's still in the shower or tub (but if not, be ready to wipe down your bathroom later—remember, you did close the door, so he shouldn't be running all over the house). Then towel dry the dog. Most dogs love this part and forget all about the indignity of the bath. (Okay, maybe not.) Keep Rover out of drafts until he's completely dry, and then revel in the joy of a clean hound.

Full Body Shake

As anyone who has ever washed a dog knows, a full-body shake begins at the nose, moves through the midsection to the rear and ends with tail flapping. A word to the uninitiated: if you are washing a dog and he begins to shake, if you can stop the head movement, sometimes you can avoid getting soaked.

Leto the Large has the most impressive body shake of our four dogs. Perhaps because he's the largest dog in the pack, it's easier to see the entire shaking process as it moves down his body and through his tail. He sort of looks like a furry zipper or something. The final tail wiggles are particularly amusing.

I've been trying for years to teach my dogs to shake on command, but so far, no dice. The idea is that you say, "shake" when the dog is wet and is going to shake himself anyway. So far my dogs have never made the connection. Oh well, at least they look really happy when they do it. Sometimes it's good to just let a dog be a dog.

Stink Dawg

As most of us have noticed, canines often do have a particular "doggie" odor. However, anything extreme may indicate a medical problem.

Before you drag Rover off to the vet, you should first consider environmental conditions. For example, we knew a guy who had a black Lab that he affectionately referred to as Stink Dawg because she smelled like a swamp. Stink Dawg had a good reason for being stinky, however; she went swimming in a pond every afternoon. As a result, she smelled like the Creature from the Black Lagoon. And, of course, if your dog has played tag with a skunk or had big fun rolling in a dead animal carcass, you can pretty much guess that she won't smell fine afterward.

If there's no environmental reason for your dog to smell bad, especially right after being cleaned, you should consider medical conditions. The dog may have a problem with his anal glands or some type of skin problem. For example, when I was growing up, we had a seriously stinky dog named Judge who smelled bad because of skin problems resulting from an unusual form of mange. (It was a good thing Judge was a nice dog because he definitely brought his own particular aura to a room.)

Bacterial or yeast infections are behind most common skin problems that cause odor. So Judge's stink factor probably was from the secondary infections, not the mange itself. The end result was that we spent a lot of time at the vet and had to dip poor Judge in many vile fluids.

Fortunately, veterinary medicine has advanced considerably since Judge's day. Veterinarians have a lot more options when it comes to treating skin problems. If your dog has red itchy skin that smells bad, she may have a yeast infection. These infections are often a side effect of allergies. To diagnose your dog, the vet may need to take a few skin samples and send them out to a lab.

If your dog has a bacterial infection, the treatment is often antibiotics and various shampoos to treat the area topically. Unfortunately, treating skin problems can be tricky because like us, dogs scratch when they itch. But you can't explain to a dog why he shouldn't scratch. It can take quite a bit of patience and treatment to clear up skin infections. However, your reward will be a dog that no longer causes an olfactory event as he walks by.

Canine Pedicure

If you are like most people, you probably don't think much about your dog's feet. But that clickety-clackety noise your dog makes as he wanders around probably means his toenails are long. Many dogs never need their nails trimmed if they walk on rough surfaces such as concrete. However, in wintertime, when there is snow on the ground and nothing to wear down their nails, I've noticed that my dogs' nails seem to get enormous quickly. Trimming your dog's nails is important because if they get too long it can cause discomfort and pain (not to mention what they can do to your floors).

If you've never trimmed your dog's nails, the prospect can be daunting. Speaking as one who owns four dogs, I know I dread it. But it must be done. You can use a couple of types of trimming tools. One type looks like miniature pliers and uses a scissor action. Another more common type uses a replaceable sliding "guillotine" blade. Either one works, but be sure that the blade is sharp before you begin.

When you trim nails, a lot depends on the dog. Two of my dogs are extremely cooperative. I tell the dog to sit, pick up the closest paw, and start trimming. However, two of my dogs are less thrilled with the idea. In cases like this, find a friend to hold the dog while you trim.

When you trim the nail, clip off only the end. Dogs have nerve endings and blood vessels inside their nails called a quick. If your dog has light colored nails, the quick looks like a dark line. You do not want to accidentally trim so close that you hit the quick. It can be difficult to see the quick on dogs with dark nails. So be very careful and trim off just a little bit at a time. If you accidentally clip too much, the quick will bleed. If this happens, apply pressure to the tip of the nail or dab on some styptic power. When it's over, give the dog a treat, pet him, and tell him how wonderful he is. With any luck, next time will be easier.

The Ears Have It

If your dog has been spending an inordinate amount of time with her foot in her ear or is shaking her head a lot, the problem may be an ear infection. As the owner of four floppy-eared dogs, I can report that ear infections are a common problem.

Your dog doesn't "catch" an ear infection from another dog. Usually, there is an underlying reason for the infection. Some dogs are just more likely to get chronic ear infections than others. Often infections develop when moisture remains in the ear so bacteria and yeast can move in. A dog may be susceptible to ear infections simply because of the shape of his ears or due to health problems such as allergies, parasites, or a hormonal imbalance such as hypothyroidism. Some dogs that live in humid environments or love to swim also may be prone to infections.

Given that infections thrive in a closed, moist environment, dogs with big floppy ears are the most likely to get infections because the ear canal is covered by the ear flap. Basset hounds are notorious for having terrible problems with ear infections, so owners of this breed have to be especially vigilant.

To check your dog's ears, lift up the flap and see if the ear canal looks dirty. Also check the smell (yes, the smell) of the ear. Many ear infections give off a particularly peculiar odor, so if the dog's ear "smells funny" it's time to head off to the veterinarian. If there's an active infection, the vet may give you antibiotics to put in the dog's ear. To prevent recurrence, he may also prescribe a drying agent to keep down the moisture level in the ear canal.

If your dog gets recurrent ear infections, you should take some preventative measures to keep your dog's ears healthy. Your vet can show you the best way to clean your dog's ears. Usually, the vet will give you an ear cleaning solution and recommend that you use a cotton ball or swab to remove any debris. Be very sure not to go deep into the ear canal; stay on the external surfaces you can see. Also never point the swab toward the dog's head; keep it pointed down toward the ground. As long as you can see the cotton part of the swab while you're cleaning, it should be safe. You don't want to damage the dog's ear in your effort to clean it.

Like anything else, overdoing ear care can be just as bad as no care at all. But if your dog starts shaking his head or scratching, check the ears. By paying attention to your dog and following your veterinarian's advice, you should be rewarded with a dog who has healthy ears.

The Houseguests You Don't Want

When cold weather starts to arrive, you may get a few unpleasant houseguests: fleas. Just because "flea season" is supposed to be over does not necessarily mean that the fleas go away. Often, they just move inside. Of course, in some warm areas, *every* season is flea season.

If you have dogs, fleas may be hitching a ride inside your home, so they can enjoy a more comfortable environment. Fleas can reportedly jump as high as 13 feet, so it's easy for a flea to jump on your dog or cat and come inside. With that in mind, you should check your pets regularly for signs of fleas.

When you check for fleas, look at the warmest parts of your dog, such as the underside where the back legs meet the body. Even if you don't find an actual flea, you may find evidence, such as eggs or "flea dirt." Fleas live off the blood of your pet and flea dirt is the partially digested blood they excrete.

It's easy to tell flea dirt from regular dirt. Just put some on a flat surface and add a drop of water. If the dirt turns red, you know it's flea dirt. Another thing you may or may not find is flea eggs, which are white and about the size of a grain of sand.

If you find evidence of fleas on your dog, the fleas are in your house as well. Fleas start laying eggs within the first 48 hours of their first meal. They can lay 40 to 50 eggs per day, and a female flea can produce more than 2,000 eggs during her lifetime. Even though not every flea survives, this tremendous ability to reproduce means that you never have "just a couple fleas."

To deal with a flea problem, you absolutely must treat every pet in your household. You need to treat the pets, the house, and the yard at the same time. If you don't, the fleas just relocate.

In the last few years, many advances have been made in flea treatments. Products exist that make it possible for you to successfully treat your pets, house, and yard safely and effectively. To find out which products would work best for your dog and your environment, consult your veterinarian for specific product recommendations and options.

Hair, Hair Everywhere

Given how many people take animals to shelters "because the dog/cat sheds," apparently people need help dealing with pet hair. Know that sharing your house with a dog means you will live with a lot of fur. Either accept that idea or don't get a dog. For those people who understand that yes, the dog will shed, here are a few suggestions for dealing with dog hair. (However, keep in mind that I'm not a neatnik, and no one would ever call my house a model of cleanliness.)

The first suggestion should be pretty obvious: brush your dog. Taking the hair off the dog keeps it from falling on the floor. I'd also like to point out that shorthaired and small animals still shed. The idea that shorthaired animals shed less is a lie. When I was growing up, we had a Labrador mix that shed vast quantities of hair year round. Yes, the individual strands may have been shorter than those of a golden retriever, but he made up for it in volume. (My rotund, shorthaired tabby cat is another example of a small animal with a tremendous amount of fur.)

If you don't want hair in a particular place, you need to keep the dog off it. The most hair collects in the places where your dog spends the most time. For example, if your gray dog has decided that the sofa is way nicer than his bed, a great gray wad of hair will collect on the sofa. (The wad of hair will subsequently affix itself to your pants when you sit on the sofa.)

Obviously, to deal with pet hair, you need to vacuum. If you have a lot of pets, it means you need a heavy-duty vacuum. These vacuums aren't cheap and if you have allergies, look for one with a HEPA filter. I also have a "rug rake" which helps take a bit of the load off the vacuum. A rug rake is exactly what it sounds like: a stick with a rubberized rake on the end that you drag across the carpet. They are usually used by folks who clean carpets. I got mine from a carpet supply store on the Internet.

You can use many things to remove hair from your clothes, like those tape roller things. However, my favorite is the old-fashioned lint brushes that catch the hair when you drag them one direction and release it when you drag it the other way. I also use the brush on furniture, when I don't want to deal with the vacuum.

Hair is a fact of life for pet owners. But with a little effort you can lower the flying fur level, even when it seems like all your pets are "blowing coat" at the same time.

CAMI

The GURP

Periodically, I have to embark on the Great Undercoat Removal Program (or GURP for short). In the spring, the canines have a tuftiness problem when it's time for all that old winter hair to go.

I have four different brushes I use for the GURP. There's a standard "slicker" brush that I rarely use, except for tails. Then there's a smallish brush with a wooden handle and only about 10 "teeth." That brush is a good starter brush to use when a dog is sort of a mess and you want to determine exactly how much hair is falling off that animal. After a few strokes with this brush to pull out the most egregious tangles and hair, it's time for the shedding brush, a.k.a., the brush that gets hair all over you.

Using the shedding brush, you can pull out vast swaths of hair. The hair sort of comes off in waves. Many waves end up on you and stay there. I tend to look like some kind of sickly sheep after brushing Cami, the extremely fuzzy white dog.

After I can't stand inhaling any more hair with the shedding brush, I move to the shedding comb. This tool requires patience. It takes a long time to comb four very hairy dogs. Fortunately, unlike the shedding brush, the hair stays on the comb until you pull it off.

After a successful GURP, it generally looks like 50 albino hamsters exploded on the floor. Cami has the thickest undercoat and the hamster pile means I've gotten most of her undercoat out. Afterward, she looks quite relaxed and happy. I end up coughing up hairballs, however.

Health Care

A healthy dog is always easier to live with than an unhealthy dog. Many behavior problems are related to chronic pain, intestinal parasites or disease, chemical or nutritional imbalances, or neurological problems. If your adopted dog was undernourished, injured, or experienced severe physical trauma like exposure to extreme cold, you might need to pay extra attention to your dog's health and work closely with your vet.

In this section, you learn about some common (and not so common) canine health issues, and what to do if your beloved pooch gets sick.

Choosing a Vet

When you get a dog, one of the first things you need to do is find a veterinarian. If you've adopted a puppy, you need a vet to give all those important vaccinations and also to get your furry friend off on the right paw medically. Even if you've adopted an adult dog, you should take her to the veterinarian for a checkup at least once a year.

The next obvious question is how do you find a veterinarian if you've just moved to a new town or you've never had a pet before? Of course, first you can check the local yellow pages to see who is out there. Many listings give you an address so you can determine if the vet clinic is near your house. It's not just a convenience issue; your proximity to the vet clinic can make a difference if you have a veterinary emergency.

You also can look online for vet clinics. Various vet locator sites exist and many veterinarians have their own Web sites these days, so you can learn a little about their facility from the convenience of your keyboard. If you adopted your dog from an animal shelter, they may also provide a list of local veterinarians.

(Often they are prohibited from actually recommending a specific clinic, however.)

The best way to find a veterinarian is to just ask around. Odds are good that someone you know has animals, so they'll undoubtedly have opinions on veterinarians. (When we moved here, one of our cats was sick, so we got a recommendation from the realtor who sold us our house.)

After you've made a selection, you may want to go to the clinic without your critter first to talk to the vet and check out the facility. Many vets will let you set up an "informational" appointment like this so they can get to know you. This visit is your chance to check out the clinic. Is it clean? What do you think of the staff? Are the other animals there totally freaked out or just (naturally) nervous? How does the vet seem to treat the other patients and staff?

Of course, you may find that your neighbors were wrong and you don't like the vet they recommended. Just because someone else says they love a particular veterinarian doesn't mean that vet is right for you. Veterinarians are people and sometimes people get along and sometimes they don't. If you feel intimidated or uncomfortable in any way, you probably should keep looking.

When you establish a good relationship with your veterinarian, you should be partners with a common goal: your dog's health. So you always want to understand what your vet is telling you. Ask questions and keep asking until you understand the medical advice he or she is giving you. Vets see your dog for only a few minutes, so they rely heavily on information from the owner to diagnose problems. Your dog can't say what hurts, so your observations are important. If you can't communicate well with the vet, your dog is the one who loses.

Taking the time to find a veterinarian you like and who will care for your dog is time well spent. Assuming your dog lives a long healthy life, you may get to know your veterinarian very well.

Pets Need Physicals Too

Many people avoid going to the doctor, except when they are sick. But even if you won't take yourself in for a physical, you should take your dog in for a veterinary exam at least once a year. Unlike a human, a dog can't tell you when he's not feeling well. Dogs are often incredibly stoic about pain, so you may not realize there is a problem until it is quite advanced. As with people, early detection is key to treating many illnesses. Plus, dogs have a much shorter life span than humans and a lot can change in just one year.

The bottom line is that making that effort to get your dog in for his annual physical is the single most important thing you can do to maintain his health, so don't put it off. Many veterinarians also give vaccinations during the annual exam. But other than shots, what exactly is the vet doing when he peers and pokes around Rover?

Vets have special training to detect subtle changes that may indicate illness. Generally, during the exam, the veterinarian will listen to the dog's heart and lungs, look in the mouth, eyes, and ears, and palpate the body to look for any unusual lumps or bumps.

At the same time, the veterinarian will ask you about any changes you've observed in your dog's behavior. Don't be afraid to bring up even small things. You see your dog every day, and it's easy to overlook small differences over time unless you pay attention. If there have been any changes in eating habits, weight gain or loss, vomiting, coughing, sneezing, or behavioral changes, be sure to report them to your veterinarian. Even if something seems a little "odd," or your dog is acting "funny" in any way, tell your vet.

Depending on your dog's health history, the veterinarian may also suggest "blood work" to screen for certain diseases and organ functions. Yearly blood screens can help your vet spot various problems before they become serious. The vet may also recommend heartworm tests and a fecal exam to check for worms or other parasites.

As your dog ages, your vet may suggest more frequent exams. Since every year of a dog or cat's life is equivalent to between 5 and 10 human years, pets over the age of 6 or so may develop age-related problems that can progress quickly. Just as a 40-year-old human shouldn't wait 10 years to have a physical, 6-year-old Rover may need to go to the vet's office more than once a year.

You and your vet are on the same team: you both want to see your dog live the longest, healthiest life possible. Getting your dog in for his physical exam is the best way to prevent or treat potentially devastating diseases. The best medicine is always preventative medicine. At the exam, the vet can diagnose and treat problems early, so you can enjoy life with your furry friend as long as possible.

LETO

Help Your Vet Help Your Dog

Two of my dogs have had cases that my vet basically couldn't figure out. Leto, my (non-Samoyed) dog that I got through Samoyed rescue, had some digestive problems probably related to being starved. Officially his diagnosis was lymphocytic plasmacystic enteritis, which basically means that his intestines were damaged so he couldn't heal himself. Anyway, the standard treatment is a drug called metronidazole.

Unfortunately, Leto had a (very rare) reaction to the drug. There's a "slight chance" of neurological side effects, which means that the dog starts staggering around. My vet had never seen the side effect in 19 years of practice. I'd read about it, so I suspected the problem. It's scary, but nothing permanent. But poor Leto couldn't take the drug anymore.

So, when conventional medicine failed, we had to move on. My vet wasn't optimistic, but recommended trying "medium chain triglycerides" (MCT) which sort of digest instantly. The idea was to help Leto put on weight and heal himself. I also gave Leto two pills. One was Acidophilus, an enzyme which is very easy to find in health food stores. The other one is a pill with digestive enzymes in it called Super Digestaway, which contains pancreatin, ox bile extract, papain (from papaya), peppermint, ginger, pepsin, betaine HCl, bromelain (from pineapple), and aloe vera gel.

After a few months on this regime, Leto looked like a new dog. A healthier, larger, furrier one. The vet actually didn't recognize him.

My second problem dog is Cami. She became extremely phobic and submissive at around 5–6 months old. I got her at 9 weeks and she was the most well adjusted little puppy I'd ever seen. But later, she started having problems with submissive urination, lick granulomas, inexplicable fears of odd things, and other erratic behavior. I had her behavior evaluated by the University of Washington Veterinary College and tried endless behavior modification techniques, drugs (amitriptyline and Clomicalm), and acupuncture. My vet and I both ran out of ideas. Nothing worked.

Then I read a reference to research being done on the link between thyroid and behavior. I went and found the original articles by Dr. Jean Dodds (such as http://www.canine-epilepsy-guardian-angels.com/bizarre_behavior.htm), which explain the correlation.

I called my vet, showed him my research and we got Cami tested. Lo and behold, the tests showed that she was, in fact, hypothyroid. She's on medication and a much happier hound now.

We're all a lot happier too. So the moral of the story is don't give up. If your critter has a problem, do some research and keep your eyes and ears alert for information that can help. Not all information is created equal (especially online), so only trust information from reputable veterinary sources. But armed with quality information, you might just surprise your vet!

Fat Dogs

Statistics show that being overweight is one of the worst things you can do to your health. Not surprisingly, obesity isn't good for your dog either. With your dog, however, you need to remember that every excess pound he gains is a greater percentage of his overall weight. If a 170-pound man gains 5 pounds it's a much smaller percentage of his weight than if a 35-pound dog gains 5 pounds. In other words, it doesn't take very many extra pounds to start causing health problems for your dog.

As in humans, dogs that are overweight have a shorter life span and experience more medical problems than dogs that are normal weight. So, how fat is too fat for your dog? If your dog is starting to look rotund, you may want to call your vet. Most veterinarians have weight charts that show the weight ranges for the various breeds of dogs.

If Fido is packing extra pounds, realize that dogs haven't figured out how to open the refrigerator (yet) so the reason he's too fat is because you fed him too much or didn't give him enough exercise. Or both. The only way to reverse the trend is to feed him less and exercise him more. You also might want to pay attention to where Fido's food is coming from. If he's scoring extra calories from treats, doggie biscuits, the cat's food bowl, and the tidbits the kids give him under the dinner table, you'll need to nix these food sources.

To help your dog lose weight, you also must increase his activity level. Even if your dog spends all day outside, he may not be doing anything more than sleeping, so he needs you to take him for a walk or inspire him to participate in a game of "fetch."

However, if your dog is seriously overweight, be sure to have your dog checked by your favorite veterinarian before embarking on any weight loss program.

Why Vaccinate

Vaccinating your dog is an important part of responsible pet ownership. It's an inexpensive way to protect your dog from a number of serious diseases. The most common vaccines are rabies, bordetella (kennel cough), and a combination vaccine that protects the dog from distemper, hepatitis, leptospirosis, parainfluenza, parvovirus, and sometimes other diseases as well.

Most people are familiar with the rabies vaccine, since it's the law that dogs must be vaccinated against rabies. These laws exist for a good reason, because rabies is a viral disease that is deadly for both people and animals. Vaccinating your dog for rabies is important for your protection, your dog's protection, and the protection of the entire community.

Bordetella, or kennel cough, is the canine equivalent of the common cold. Like a cold, the infection is contagious, and dogs who come in contact with other dogs at boarding kennels, dog shows, or even veterinary clinics may be at risk of contracting the disease. Unfortunately, another similarity with the common cold is that bordetella isn't caused by just one germ. Dogs with weakened immune systems from other viruses are most susceptible to infection. Most boarding kennels or obedience classes will require you to show proof of bordetella vaccination.

The combination vaccine protects against a number of terrible diseases. Distemper is a potentially fatal viral disease that affects the dog's respiratory, gastrointestinal, and nervous systems. Canine hepatitis is a viral disease of the liver, and leptospirosis is a bacterial disease that affects the liver and kidneys. Parainfluenza is another common cause of canine coughing, and parvovirus is an extremely serious viral disease that damages a dog's intestinal lining.

Although all puppies should have a complete set of shots, some veterinarians now prefer to cater a dog's later vaccinations to the dog's lifestyle. Talk to your veterinarian about what is best for your dog.

Boarding and Bordetella

If you will be taking your dog to a boarding kennel, you should take your dog to the vet first. In addition to the standard vaccinations, virtually all boarding kennels require that you also get your dog vaccinated against bordetella or "kennel cough." Any time your dog will be in close proximity to other dogs, such as at dog shows, classes, or boarding kennels, it's a good idea to take him to the vet for a bordetella vaccination first.

As mentioned earlier about the common cold in humans, more than one organism may cause kennel cough or infectious tracheobronchitis. However, the majority of cases are caused by a bacterial infection that includes infection by an organism called *Bordetella bronchiseptica*, so the terms bordetella and kennel cough are often used interchangeably.

Although humans aren't affected by bordetella, among dogs it can be extremely contagious because it spreads by coughed droplets. Although it's possible for a dog to be infected by another dog that is some distance away, dogs are most likely to be exposed to germs in a place where there are a lot of other dogs, much like kids who go to kindergarten and get sick from exposure to a lot of other children. If a dog is already physically or emotionally stressed in some way, he's also more likely to become ill.

Again, like a human cold, generally kennel cough isn't a severe problem. But it's definitely unpleasant for both dog and owner. The disease is characterized by dry hacking coughing fits that sound like the dog has smoked three packs of cigarettes. Often a coughing jag is followed by gagging or retching, so you may think that the dog has something stuck in his throat. The dog may have a fever, be listless, vomit, or lose his appetite. In rare cases, kennel cough actually can lead to pneumonia or other serious problems.

Because kennel cough can be caused by infection from several viruses, some vets don't treat it with antibiotics. However, some do use antibiotics to prevent any secondary bacterial infections. Often a cough suppressant is prescribed to make the dog more comfortable.

As with most diseases, if prevention is possible, it's far preferable to treatment after the fact. Two types of vaccines exist for bordetella: intranasal and injectable. The intranasal vaccine is administered directly into the dog's nose, and it generally acts more quickly than the injectable version. The injectable version may provide longer immunity however.

Even the intranasal vaccine takes around four or five days to provide complete protection, so if you plan to board your dog, schedule that appointment for a vaccination today.

Doggie Dental Care

Many people don't think about their dog's dental health, but it's important. Although dogs don't often get cavities, the plaque and tartar on their teeth can cause gingivitis and periodontal disease. Without treatment the teeth can decay and eventually fall out. Veterinarians see many a toothless dog whose owners ignored doggie dental care.

Healthy teeth aren't just a cosmetic nicety. Another less obvious side effect comes from the bacteria that cause the decay. These bacteria can actually travel through the dog's bloodstream and damage major organs. Dogs with bad teeth can become very sick.

When it comes to dental care, prevention is important. Just as you go to the dentist regularly (we hope), you should take your dog in for regular dental checkups at the veterinarian. Almost any time you take your dog into the vet, you've probably noticed the vet checks the dog's teeth. He's looking for yellowy, crusty tartar and plaque on the teeth, and red along the gum line that indicates gingivitis.

If your vet finds problems, he or she will let you know that it's time for a cleaning. Called a dental prophy, or prophylaxis, this procedure is a thorough cleaning and polishing of your dog's teeth. The dog needs to be anesthetized for the procedure, although many vets do let the dog go home the same day.

Afterward, the veterinarian may recommend home tooth brushing. I confess that, personally, even though I floss my own teeth every night, I've had zero success with brushing my dogs' teeth. I accept my limitations and realize that it means I have to take the canine team in for teeth cleanings more frequently than if I regularly brushed their teeth myself.

If brushing the dog's teeth isn't working out, your vet may recommend specially formulated foods that help reduce the accumulation of plaque and tartar. Various treats and chew toys also may help. Generally, large dogs who eat dry food and engage in lots of recreational chewing are less susceptible to periodontal disease than small dogs. Small breeds like Pomeranians and Pekingese are particularly at risk for tooth problems because their teeth are crowded more tightly and prone to more plaque buildup.

If you take your dog in for yearly exams, don't be surprised if you hear what I did when I took my dog Cami in last time. "Look at those teeth! Yuck. It's time for a cleaning!" Since we want Cami to be around for a long time, she headed back to the vet shortly afterward for some important dental care.

Post Surgical Pet Care

After you bring your dog home from spay, neuter, or other type of surgery, you need to give your furry friend a little extra TLC. Often the veterinarian will give you post-surgical advice, but in the excitement of bringing Fido home, it's easy to forget what they told you.

When you bring your dog home, she may be a bit sleepy or groggy from the anesthetic. Some types of anesthetic may make your dog drool or seem more uncoordinated than usual. Anesthetic also can cause nausea, so the evening after surgery, you should give the dog access to water, but avoid feeding.

As caretaker, your job is to keep your dog as comfortable and quiet as possible so she can heal. If you have kids or pets, keep them from bothering the patient for at least 24 hours. For three to five days, it's best to keep the patient indoors because you want to keep your dog or cat away from excessive hot, cold, or wet weather. In other words, right after surgery, you really shouldn't just throw the dog outside in the yard or let the cat out to roam the neighborhood.

While your dog is healing, be sure she avoids strenuous exercise or play. You should check the incision area twice a day and look for any bleeding, excessive swelling, redness, odor, or drainage. Some minor swelling and redness may occur, but contact your vet if you see a wide gap or tissue protruding from the incision.

It's also important to keep your dog from licking or chewing at the incision, no matter how much she may want to fuss at it. This type of excessive attention can result in torn stitches, slow healing, or infection. (If the dog is successful in ripping out the stitches, you may need to bring her in for another surgery!) Some critters absolutely won't stop licking, so you may have to either buy or borrow an "Elizabethan collar" or E-collar.

A number of types of E-collars are available, but the traditional type is essentially a large plastic cone that fits over your dog's head. Pretty much every animal that has ever worn one hates it. The annoyed patient may bang into walls, furniture, doors, the floor, and you. She may give you dirty looks and appear completely morose. Don't feel guilty! It's important that you don't take off the E-collar, unless you can keep an eagle eye on your dog. You really don't want to have to go back to the vet for an infection or incision repair.

Depending on the surgery, your dog may or may not need to have stitches removed. If there are stitches, they generally need to remain in place for a week to ten days. After a week, the incision should be sealed. If there is no discharge, pain or redness, your dog is probably just about healed.

Assuming you've done your monitoring job well and you get the okay from your veterinarian, your post-surgical caretaker duties are over and you and your dog can go back to your normal routine.

LEIA

Miss Cone Head

Recently I had a dog epiphany: when you own four dogs, it's really dumb to not have an E-collar. This revelation came to me one day when I looked down at my black dog, Leia, and noticed that she was furiously rubbing at her face. Her left eye was red and angry looking.

Poor Leia definitely had something going on with her eye and she just wouldn't leave it alone. All that rubbing was making the problem worse, but you can't explain that to a dog. After I called the vet and begged for an early appointment, we looked all over the house for an E-collar substitute. Normally you use an E-collar to keep the critter from licking himself. But in this case, I wanted the opposite effect. I wanted an E-collar so Leia couldn't rub her eye with her paw.

In any case, our search through the house was fruitless. In the past, I've read you can make some sort of quasi-effective E-collar using a bucket, but that approach didn't look very promising, given the materials available.

For a while, my husband James and I took turns holding onto Leia to keep her from rubbing. Eventually, I put a bandana over her eye. She really didn't appreciate the pirate look one little bit. However, she did lie down on the floor looking sad and left her eye alone until it was time to go to the vet.

The excitement of the car ride kept her busy as well. Yet the first words out of my mouth after we got to the clinic was, "how much is an E-collar?"

Heartworm Disease

Heartworm disease affects dogs and cats and is spread by mosquitoes. It is one of those diseases that is easy to prevent, but difficult to cure. A worm called *Dirofilaria immitis* causes the disease. Part of its life cycle involves living in a mosquito. The infective larvae of the worm are injected into the animal when an infected mosquito bites the dog or cat. Heartworm is most common in tropical areas where the most mosquitoes live, but it is present in almost all areas of the United States and parts of Canada. If you've seen mosquitoes, you should talk to your vet about heartworm.

Although both cats and dogs can get heartworm, it's most common in dogs. The worm lives in the blood vessels of the infected animal so heartworm is diagnosed using a blood screening test. In the early stages, a dog may not show any symptoms of the disease. As it progresses, the heart becomes more and more stressed. Dogs start to experience problems with breathing and have an unwillingness to exercise. They may also cough, lose weight, and become listless and depressed.

Treatment for cats is difficult and often can be fatal, however dogs with heartworm often recover. The most important part of the treatment happens at home. Basically a vet gives the dog drugs to kill the worm. As the worms die, they travel through the bloodstream. If blockages occur, they can kill the dog. So a dog undergoing heartworm treatment absolutely has to avoid any form of exercise, or even may need to be confined to a kennel for about a month. The dog must be kept quiet so the body can break down and absorb the dying worms.

Although heartworm is a terrible disease, preventing it is quite simple. Your veterinarian can recommend different types of preventatives. Preventatives can be given monthly, daily, or as an injection that is done by your vet once every 6 months. It is important to discuss the type of chemicals that are contained in the pills or injection because certain breeds of dogs react to certain types of heartworm medications. Before you get a preventative, the vet also will need to do a blood test to determine if heartworms are already present. Dogs never should be given preventative medicine without determining whether or not heartworm is already present.

Heartworm preventatives have changed a lot over the years and continue to evolve. These days, some preventatives also work against other internal or external parasites as well. Your veterinarian can explain all the different options when you bring in your dog for the heartworm test.

Bloat

If you have a large dog, you should be aware of a digestive problem called "bloat." Bloat is the common name for a serious condition known as gastric dilatation and volvulus (GDV), which is one of the leading causes of death in giant dog breeds. Recognizing the symptoms of bloat is important because the dog's life depends on early treatment by a veterinarian. When a dog experiences bloat, the stomach fills with air and/or fluid and may rotate on itself. If the stomach rotates (volvulus), the blood supply is cut off and the stomach begins to die. Because of this disruption in the blood supply, the dog's condition worsens rapidly. Even with veterinary intervention, as many as 35% of the dogs that experience bloat die.

Bloat is caused by a combination of genetic and environmental factors. Certain breeds are significantly more susceptible to bloat; it is much more likely to occur in large, deep-chested breeds such as Great Danes. If you see symptoms such as non-productive vomiting after eating, anxiety, excessive salivating, whining, pacing, restlessness, labored breathing, or distention of the abdomen, you need to get the dog to a vet immediately. In the advanced stages of bloat, especially if the stomach has twisted, the dog's gums will be dark red, blue, gray, or white, and the dog will have a rapid heartbeat and a weak pulse. At this stage, death is imminent.

You can reduce the likelihood of bloat by taking the following precautions:

- Feed the dog two or three times a day, rather than once a day.

- Limit water immediately after feeding.

- Make sure the dog avoids vigorous exercise one hour before and two hours after eating.

- Feed the dog in a quiet location.

- Know the symptoms of bloat and if you suspect a problem, call your vet ASAP.

Because of the genetic factor, even if you take the precautions above, your dog may still experience bloat. If you have a large dog, talk to your veterinarian about what you can do to minimize your dog's risk.

Canine Pancreatitis

Pancreatitis is a serious but not uncommon problem in dogs. Basically, when the pancreas becomes inflamed and essentially starts digesting itself, that disorder is called pancreatitis. As most veterinarians will tell you, they see a lot of pancreatitis cases around the holidays because it often flares up after the dog has consumed an extremely rich, fatty meal. The classic problem is that the dog gets into the Thanksgiving turkey, gorges on it, and then gets very sick. However, sometimes pancreatitis comes on for no apparent reason.

The symptoms of pancreatitis are varied. It depends on the dog. Some dogs become depressed and lethargic. Generally, they vomit, have diarrhea, fever, and abdominal pain. In really severe attacks, the dog may actually go into shock and die. The side effects also can be worse than pancreatitis itself, including blood clotting, heart, liver, or kidney problems.

Because the only way to "rest" the pancreas is to avoid food, if they suspect pancreatitis, most vets will suggest that you avoid giving your dog food or water for 24 to 72 hours. Sometimes owners can actually contribute to the problem. Rover stops eating one night, so the solicitous owner gives the dog a little something "special" in his food, like tasty table scraps. Rover then starts vomiting everywhere and an emergency vet trip ensues.

Unfortunately a diagnosis of pancreatitis can be difficult to determine. Sometimes the diagnosis comes simply from ruling out other possibilities. Usually the vet will do a blood test. If the levels that show kidney and liver function or white blood cell count are elevated, they may indicate pancreatitis. Sometimes the vet may do x-rays or ultrasound tests to rule out other possible problems that cause abdominal pain, such as intestinal obstructions.

A severe bout of pancreatitis may require hospitalization because the dog can become seriously dehydrated. So the vet will put the dog on fluids and often provide pain-relief drugs as well. Some dogs only have one bout of pancreatitis over their entire lifetime. In fact, a dog we had when I was growing up was hospitalized for pancreatitis and never had another problem.

However, for some dogs, the problem can become chronic and pancreatitis returns repeatedly. You can help prevent reoccurrence to some degree by keeping your dog's weight down and avoiding table scraps. Your vet may also be able to recommend special foods that may help. Because it can vary from essentially a mild stomachache to a fatal illness, pancreatitis is not something to be taken lightly.

Arthritis

As they get older, many dogs suffer from arthritis. The term arthritis refers to inflammation of the joints and symptoms include joint pain and stiffness. If your dog no longer romps up the stairs and seems to get up slowly and carefully, he probably has some degree of joint pain.

Certain breeds of dogs are more likely to get arthritis. Obese dogs also have a much greater risk of developing arthritis than their lean canine counterparts. If your dog has ever had a problem in any joints, such as hip dysplasia, or trauma such as a broken bone, the risk of arthritis is greater.

For example, my dog Tika was found frozen into the ice in downtown Sandpoint, Idaho when she was a tiny puppy. When I adopted her at 5 months, the vet warned me that Tika was likely to become arthritic later in life because of this early trauma and because of her breed. Golden retrievers like Tika often get arthritis, and now that Tika is about 6 years old, she is definitely a little stiff in the mornings.

Dogs also can be predisposed to arthritis if they've had certain infections, such as Lyme disease, so it's a good idea to watch out for ticks. Many canines are rather stoic about pain, but if you see your dog limping or he has difficulty moving around or sensitivity to being touched, you should talk to your veterinarian.

Veterinarians see a lot of dogs with arthritis, and fortunately, a number of treatments are now available. For years, vets have prescribed low doses of aspirin for dogs to help manage pain. Now other arthritis drugs are available, such as Rimadyl, Deramaxx, and EtoGesic. All three are nonsteroidal anti-inflammatory drugs or NSAIDs, which are designed to reduce inflammation and pain.

When you talk to your vet about drug treatments, be sure you get information about possible side effects. Rimadyl toxicity is somewhat rare, but potentially fatal. The last thing you want to do is kill your dog with kindness, so read the drug package inserts and always follow your vet's advice as far as dosage.

You also can help make your dog more comfortable by making simple changes like providing a soft bed. A bed with extra padding is a lot easier on joints than sleeping on a cold hard floor. If your dog is fat, putting him on a diet will also help. Regular exercise keeps the muscles and ligaments in good shape.

As with humans, massage can help ease stiffness and increase circulation, so your dog feels better. Doggie massage isn't just relaxing for the dog either. Basically, giving your dog a massage is an excuse to pet all that great canine fur a little more than usual, which is good for you too.

Canine Epilepsy and Seizures

Seizures are scary. As you helplessly look on, your dog's neurological system seems to go haywire. A seizure is actually a symptom, not a disease itself. Basically, sudden abnormal electrical activity in the brain causes uncontrollable behavior or actions such as convulsions. In a dog, a seizure may range from just a facial twitching to the dog falling over on his side paddling his paws.

Brain tumors, low blood sugar, thyroid disorders, poisoning, and a host of other conditions may cause seizures, so if your dog has a seizure, you should call your veterinarian as soon as you can. If your dog has quickly repeating or extended seizures, he may require emergency medical attention.

During the seizure, do not try to "help" your dog by opening his mouth or restraining him. You could easily hurt yourself or the dog in the process. During the seizure, the dog won't respond to you, but do try and keep any objects out of his way. After the seizure, the dog may be frightened and disoriented. Talk to him in a soft voice and try to reassure him. Keep him calm and away from the stairs and other obstacles for a while until you are sure he has really recovered and can walk around without stumbling.

Although the seizure may feel almost as stressful for you as it is for the dog, try to pay attention to what's going on. Be sure to note exactly what happened before, during, and after the seizure, so you can report this information to your veterinarian. Dogs may have only one seizure in their entire life or may have conditions such as epilepsy that are characterized by multiple seizures. Pay attention to anything that might have triggered the seizure. Triggers can include stress, certain foods or ingredients, or even noises.

When you take your dog to the vet, he will probably do a whole range of tests to try and find a cause for the seizures. However, many seizures fall into the "idiopathic" category, which means they have no known cause. Even if your vet can't figure out why the seizure happens, he still can offer treatments. A number of medications are available that can help control seizures. The two most commonly prescribed medications are phenobarbital and bromide. You will want to be conscientious about giving the medications and work closely with your veterinarian to monitor your dog's response to the medications and watch for potential side effects. Anecdotal evidence suggests that diet changes can help seizures as well, so you may want to talk to your vet about possible changes you can make to your dog's food.

Although seizures are an upsetting experience for both dogs and their owners, with medication and TLC, you can help your dog live a long and happy life.

Licking, Biting, and Chewing

Most people have seen dogs scratching and biting themselves. Generally the assumption is that the dog has an itch. But sometimes the scratching and biting can become destructive, so that the dog actually injures himself. Excessive licking can start a cycle that is hard to break as the dog's licking and biting leads to a lesion on his skin that gets infected. This, in turn, causes the dog to lick even more, resulting in more hair loss and skin damage.

The causes of self-mutilation can stem from relatively common medical problems or psychological conditions. Allergies are a common reason dogs scratch and bite. Your dog could be allergic to food, fleas, or some element in his environment such as molds, dust, or grasses. Treating allergies can be a complex process and you should consult with your vet for specific advice. In general with allergies, you attempt to either avoid the allergen or manage the symptoms.

For example, if the dog has a food allergy and you can isolate the ingredient that causes the problem, you can switch to a food that doesn't contain the ingredient. However, if your dog is allergic to dust or pollen, avoiding it can be difficult. In that case, your vet may recommend soothing shampoos, allergy shots, or other treatment to help manage the symptoms.

Hot spots or "acute moist dermatitis" are another problem that may cause intense itching. These red, inflamed areas are caused by a bacterial infection and can turn into a big problem as the dog causes further damage as he bites and scratches himself. Other skin infections, ear infections, or various parasites and mites can cause itching as well. For example, if you see your dog shaking his head and scratching at his ears a lot, it may indicate an ear infection. A trip to the vet is in order.

Not all licking and scratching has a medical cause however. Some cases of self-mutilation actually are a form of obsessive-compulsive disorder. Just as people may become obsessive about washing their hands, dogs may become obsessive about licking or biting themselves.

For example, acral lick dermatitis is the term for a repetitive, compulsive licking disorder that leads to skin damage, infections, and lesions on the legs or feet. Other dogs may compulsively chase their tails to the point of biting and mutilating themselves. Or dogs will lick and suck their flanks until they have no hair.

These obsessive-compulsive behaviors may begin with a medical problem. The dog has a hot spot and starts licking his leg because it itches. But even after the hot spot is healed, he still licks his leg because the licking alleviates stress. Treating obsessive-compulsive disorders is challenging. Your vet may suggest an E-collar in the short term, prescribe anti-depressant medication, or enlist the help of a behaviorist.

No matter what the cause, if your dog is licking, biting, or chewing himself, there's a problem. So talk to your vet about possible solutions. Being itchy or in pain is no fun for any dog.

LEIA

Endless Slurping

It's pretty quiet as I sit here writing away, but with four dogs in the house, odds are pretty good that sooner or later some canine is going to be making some revolting noise somewhere soon.

My desk faces the wall and the hounds tend to hang out on the carpet behind my chair. Even though I can't see them, I can hear them. I can report that when a longhaired dog has an itch in particularly private places, it apparently takes some serious snorfling to get through the fur and find the offending patch of itchy skin.

Even now, I hear Cami's particular snorfle-slurp as she tidies up some body part. After years of cohabitation, it's easy to tell which hound is making the disgusting noise without even turning around.

Leia, the black dog, tends to be methodical in all things. Listening to her get a drink of water is like some kind of sound torture. Slurp. Pause. Slurp. Pause. Slurp. She cleans herself in much the same methodical way.

It's amazing how close we get to our pets. Like any other family member you live with, you get to know what your pets look, sound, and smell like at all times of day or night. And hey, depending on the dog or human, that can sometimes be a sort of gross thing.

But we love them anyway.

Keeping Your Dog Safe

Because dogs are not people, they don't understand that cars are dangerous or that eating certain things can kill them. Concepts like "dangerous highway" or "toxic chemicals" just aren't part of their world. And like small children, sometimes dogs are just too busy following their nose, indulging their instincts, or just plain having fun to look where they're going... and that can get them into trouble.

This section will help you protect your dog from common canine dangers that lurk in our backyards, driveways, and homes, as well as offer some special precautions you need to take during certain seasons and holidays.

Puppy Proofing

When you get a new puppy, you need to think about things from their perspective. Like little children, they test new items by tasting them. For the safety of your new companion, you should pet proof your home. Here are a few common items you should look out for:

1. Antifreeze. Because of its sweet flavor, antifreeze is tempting. It's also extremely toxic and almost invariably fatal when ingested.

2. Various cleaning supplies, bleach, pesticides, fertilizer can all be toxic. Be sure to store them safely out of reach.

3. Electrical cords. Secure cords away from inquisitive puppy teeth or secure the puppy away from cords.

4. Automatic garage door openers. Pets are often crushed by garage doors, so check to make sure that no animals are hiding nearby before you close the door.

5. Sweets, especially chocolate, can make pets seriously ill.

6. Toys can be hazardous if they fall apart and big pieces are ingested. Carefully monitor your pet's chewing habits and take away any problematic toys.

7. Cigarette butts can cause nicotine poisoning if eaten.

8. Indoor plants. Certain house plants are poisonous, including: chrysanthemum, poinsettia, pot mums, spider mums, arrowhead vine, Boston ivy, colodium, drunk cane, philodendron, neththytis, parlor ivy, amaryllis, azalea, creeping charlie, majesty, elephant ears, Jerusalem cherry, umbrella plant, ripple ivy, mistletoe, English ivy, and narcissus.

Poisonous Outdoor Plants

Various common outdoor plants can be poisonous to your dog. Here's a list of some of them:

Daffodils, skunk cabbage, foxglove, ground cherry, soap berry, rhubarb, spinach, tomato vine, buttercup, water hemlock, mushrooms, moonseed, angel's trumpet, jasmine, morning glory, periwinkle, rhododendron, lily of the valley, nightshade, bleeding heart.

Certain trees and shrubs also can be a problem. Watch out for horse chestnut, pain tree, all types of yew, English holly, balsam pear, almond, peach, and cherry.

The issue of poisoning shouldn't be taken lightly. A friend of ours who lives in a more tropical clime had a beautiful Great Pyrenees puppy that the whole family adored. They discovered too late that the shrubs around their house were poisonous. The puppy had apparently been chomping on the leaves and died. The family subsequently had all the plants removed.

If your dog is inclined to eat plants, be sure to remove the plant or the pet, so the animal can't get at the plant. If you suspect that your dog has eaten any type of poisonous substance, be sure to contact your veterinarian immediately!

Antifreeze

Antifreeze isn't just something puppies get into. Unfortunately, although it may seem innocuous because it's so common, ethylene glycol, the active ingredient in most antifreeze and some windshield washer fluid, is a deadly poison. According to the Humane Society, tens of thousands of animals die every year due to ethylene glycol poisoning. In fact, they assert that antifreeze is one of the most dangerous household hazards to animals and children that exists.

The reason that ethylene glycol poisoning is so common is twofold. First, dogs, cats, and kids (especially young ones) investigate new things with their mouths. Everyone knows that dogs chew, cats lick, and little kids put everything into their mouths.

Second, even though it's a fatal toxin, antifreeze made with ethylene glycol is sweet and actually tastes good. A tiny amount is extremely poisonous and fatal within hours. The signs of poisoning include excessive thirst and urination, lack of coordination, weakness, nausea, tremors, vomiting, rapid breathing, rapid heart rate, convulsions, diarrhea, and paralysis.

If you suspect poisoning, you need to take your dog to the veterinarian at once to avoid an extremely swift and painful death. You can do a number of things to keep your kids and animals safe. The first and most obvious change you can make is to put a different kind of antifreeze in your car. A number of antifreeze products are now formulated with propylene glycol instead of the deadly ethylene glycol. These newer formulations work just as well as the old fashioned version, but aren't hazardous to humans or animals (and they even taste bad).

If you do use ethylene glycol-based products, be sure to keep your pets inside while you change your antifreeze. Don't spill any on the ground and if you do, clean it up immediately. Don't dump the old antifreeze into ditches or drains. You should always dispose of used antifreeze properly at a site that takes hazardous waste.

Hot Weather Tips

With the advent of warmer weather every year, you need to take a few precautions to ensure the health of your favorite furry friend. First, remember to never leave your dog alone in a vehicle. Even with the windows open, a parked car can heat up, becoming a furnace that will kill your pet in minutes. Parking in the shade may seem like a good idea, but shade shifts throughout the day and that shady spot becomes a potentially fatal sunny spot. So either leave your dogs at home or take them inside when they travel with you.

If you absolutely must leave your dog in the car however briefly, park in the shadiest spot you can find, put a sun shade up in the windshield, and invest in a set of window ventilation grilles, so you can safely leave the windows open. Even with these precautions, don't leave the dog inside the car for more than 10 minutes. Those few minutes can be the difference between life and death.

When you take Rover out for his walk, think about his comfort. If you are feeling hot, your dog probably is too. It's much better for your dog (and you) to exercise in the cool of the early morning or evening. In really hot weather, the asphalt can burn sensitive paws, since they aren't covered with shoes like your feet are. Dogs with short noses such as bulldogs, Pekingese, Boston terriers, and Lhasa apsos also tend to have special difficulties in the heat, so keep them inside during really hot weather. In the heat, it's also especially important for your pets to have access to plenty of water at all times.

If your dog gets overheated, you need to lower his body temperature. The signs of heat stress include: heavy panting, glazed eyes, rapid pulse, dizziness, vomiting, and a deep red or purple tongue. To lower the dog's temperature, find some shade and apply cool (but not cold) water over his body. You also can apply ice packs or cold towels to the head, neck, and chest. Let the dog drink small amounts of water or lick ice cubes, and be sure to get him to a veterinarian as soon as possible.

Avoid walking your dog in areas where pesticides have been sprayed. Animals are often killed or sickened by coming in contact with insecticides or poisons. Also check for antifreeze leaking from your car. It too is a potentially fatal poison. If you think your dog may have accidentally ingested a poisonous substance, contact your veterinarian immediately.

Most importantly, if you haven't already done so, put ID tags on your pets and get them "fixed." Many dogs get loose to go find a mate. The inevitable result is more lost dogs and unwanted puppies at the local animal shelter. Dogs also frequently jump out (or fall out) of vehicles. Don't let your dog become another homeless pet statistic: get an ID tag, microchip, or some form of ID on your pets ASAP.

The Bear Pool

With all that fur, our Samoyed mix, Cami, gets very hot in the summer. Her favorite way to cool off is to dunk her furry self into water. Since our house isn't located on a lake, pond, or river, we bought her one of those cheapie blue plastic baby pools you can buy at Big-Box stores for about $10. Because we call Cami "The Bear," the ugly little blue pool was immediately dubbed the Bear Pool.

The Bear Pool was probably one of the best $10 we ever spent on Cami. After a walk through the forest, Cami anxiously stands at the kennel gate. As soon as we open the door, she charges in and splashes down in her pool. She circles the perimeter of the pool and then reclines with her head hanging over the side of the pool and her tongue lolling out of her mouth.

After about 35 seconds of reclining, Cami leaps up and out of the Bear Pool. Then she sidles over to some unsuspecting human or canine and shakes a mighty shake, spraying water everywhere.

Satisfied with a job well done, Cami then sleeps and waits for all that fur to dry. The term "it's a dog's life" does not necessarily refer to hard work.

Have a Safe Fourth

During the fun and fireworks of the 4th of July, the family dog is often forgotten. All those bombs bursting in air may be a great part of the festivities for you, but they can cause a lot of stress for Rover. A lot of very scared animals end up at animal shelters after the 4th of July. Many of them have become disoriented and lost or get hurt in their panic to get away from the noise.

A frightened animal may run for hours or days, get hit by a car, or be injured directly from the fireworks themselves. Dog owners can do their part to minimize pet panic during the holiday. Make sure you don't leave your dogs outside, especially alone, while fireworks are being discharged. If your dog does get out, be sure to call the local animal shelters immediately. Shelters generally log every lost and found phone call and frequently can match owners looking for their lost pets with individuals who have found or rescued a scared and lost animal.

So before the partying begins, think of your furry friends and do the following to keep your dog safe:

1. Keep your animals inside and away from any fireworks.

2. If your dog is afraid of loud noises, he or she will undoubtedly find the sound of fireworks terrifying. Stay with your pet and make sure she is okay.

3. If you know your dog will become hyperactive, destructive, or "bolt" at all the noises, you may want to consider talking to your veterinarian about sedative-type drugs to make the experience less stressful.

4. Most importantly, ALWAYS have proper identification on your dog with your current address and phone number. Free ID tags are often available from animal shelters, so stop by and pick one up if your pet does not have an ID tag.

A little planning and thoughtfulness on your part can keep you and your dog safe and happy over the holiday.

Get Your Dog Ready for Winter

In the midst of "winter preparedness" tasks like chopping wood and taking down fencing, don't forget about your dog. Even though dogs have fur, it doesn't give them enough protection from extreme cold. If the weather gets below 10 or 20 degrees, bring the dog inside. Very young, old, or sick dogs are even less tolerant to the cold, so as temperatures drop, be sure that they have a way to stay warm.

It's also important to get your dog used to colder temperatures incrementally. If they spend some time outside throughout the fall, dogs adapt to the changing of the season by growing more fur and storing more fat. In other words: don't suddenly decide in the middle of winter that your dog is going to be an outside dog. It will be extremely hard on the dog. By giving the dog's body a chance to adapt to colder temperatures throughout fall, he'll be able to withstand winter weather more easily.

Your dog may need more food as the temperatures drop as well. If your dog starts losing weight, he'll be less able to withstand the cold, so it may be necessary to increase his food intake by as much as 25%–30% during the winter. It should be obvious, but as the temperatures drop, it's especially important to give your dog shelter. We've all seen the dogs tied to doghouses out in the cold, rain, wind, and snow. This treatment is simply cruel.

Every dog deserves to have a warm, dry place to curl up, even if he's an "outside" dog. Installing a "doggie door" into a garage or mud room can be a good solution because the door allows the dog to go inside whenever the weather turns foul, even if you aren't home to let him in. With a few common sense precautions, you can keep your dog healthy and happy throughout the winter months.

The Wood Stove Incident

The good news about our wood stove is that it does what it's supposed to do and puts out about a gazillion BTUs when we need it. The bad news is that the animals in the household haven't seemed to clue in that when the thing is on, it's really hot.

One extremely cold day last winter, I had just loaded a log into the wood stove and turned around to go get some of those stupid credit card mailers you get that need to be burned or shredded.

When I headed back toward the wood stove, I noticed a big black smear on the front glass. And a horrible, horrible smell. I realized it was hair and looked over at the black dog. Leia looked back at me as if to say "huh?"

So I looked around at the other dogs and found a singed tail. At some point, while my back was turned, Cami (not Leia) had been standing too close to the wood stove. Normally her tail curves over her back. Apparently, as she lowered her tail down, it got too close to the wood stove and was burned on the glass. There was a big mass of blackened fur on the end of her lovely white tail. The damage had obviously stopped before it got to her skin, but she still looked pretty alarmed by the hideous smell.

I got some scissors and chopped off the burned fur, which seemed to make her feel better. Intellectually, I know all that tail fur will grow back, but every time I look at her stubby and less fluffy tail tip, I think about what could have happened if she'd actually caught fire.

In any case, the next day we went and got one of those portable cages and put it around the wood stove to keep all critters away when we run it. For reasons unknown, the cage wire doesn't even get hot and it works great.

....

Do You Need to Winterize Your Dog?

Although some types of dogs are more affected by cold than others, you can do a number of things to help keep Rover's winter experience safe and happy.

1. Consider your dog. At my house, Cami, the Samoyed mutt, is not fazed by almost any level of cold. Samoyeds are very furry, white, sled-type dogs, so winter is no big deal to the wooly Cami hound. However, even though Tika, my golden retriever, could be considered fairly furry, goldens were not really bred to deal with extreme temperatures, and Tika is a cold wimp. Just because your dog has hair does not mean that she's immune to cold. Older dogs and arthritic dogs are especially sensitive to the cold. Take your dog's breed, health, age, and temperament into account when making decisions about time spent outdoors.

2. Provide shelter. If you keep your dog outside, be sure she has adequate shelter. A doghouse should be raised off the ground, dry, and free of drafts. If the house is heated, have the wiring done professionally. Extension cords and space heaters are not a good mix around canines. If you line the doghouse with straw, be sure to change the straw when it gets wet. Area vets see far too many dogs with horrible skin rashes and respiratory problems because the dogs were forced to sleep on wet, moldy straw.

3. Provide food and water. In the winter, your dog needs extra calories to stay warm. So feed him a larger ration of good quality food. If your dog is going to spend any significant time outside, you also must provide fresh water, which may entail buying a heater for the water dish, so it doesn't freeze over.

4. Beware winter dangers. Animals can get frostbite just like humans. The ears, nose, and paws are particularly susceptible. Also watch out for any chemicals that may be on the road or sidewalks, such as de-icers. When your dog licks his feet, he may ingest these chemicals and get sick. Most importantly, keep any automotive chemicals, especially antifreeze, away from all your pets. Antifreeze poisoning is common and almost always fatal.

The bottom line is use common sense. Cold can be dangerous. Always take the wind chill into account. Even if it's 32 degrees outside, a stiff wind can drop the temperature 20 degrees or more. Pay attention to your dog. For years, I have done an unscientific "ear check" when I bring in my dogs to evaluate how cold they are. Now I have a good idea how long they can comfortably be outside at a given temperature. When the doggie ears are too cold, it's time for the canine team to come inside and do some power sleeping on the nice warm carpet.

TIKA

Tender Toes

Tika and I do not embrace the cold weather. When it is the coldest out in the early morning, the furry team walks around the doggie "outing" area like they are on tippie toes.

On one morning outing at −11 degrees (F), Cami collapsed in a little pile to mess around with the ice in her paw. Leto looked disturbed, and Leia was very, very quick about her business and ran back to the front porch.

But poor little Tika was by far the most offended by walking on the ultra cold snow. First she'd pick up one foot, then put it down and pick up another. She kept picking up various feet and all the while glaring at me like it was my fault.

I can tell you right now that a tripod hound giving you the evil eye is not a good way to start the day.

A couple of people suggested booties, but clearly they have not met Tika. We don't call her "spaz dog" for nothing. I'd give booties about 2.3 seconds before she'd have them off of those furry feet. And then she'd glare at me even more.

Holiday Treats Your Dog Shouldn't Eat

When you see those big brown puppy-dog eyes looking over at you yearning for food, it's hard to say no. But you should. Halloween is just one of a string of holidays that are filled with treats and food your dog shouldn't eat.

Many people don't realize that candy and various human foods are bad for pets. For example, chocolate can actually poison your dog. It contains caffeine and a chemical called theobromine, and in large amounts can be extremely toxic to your pet. The toxicity depends on the type of chocolate. White chocolate is the least dangerous and dark baking chocolate is the most dangerous. If your candy stash mysteriously disappears and your dog starts becoming restless and hyperactive or vomiting, get him to the veterinarian immediately. Most animals recover, but the toxicity depends on the dog's weight. If a small dog eats a lot of candy, it can be fatal.

The types of rich fatty foods dogs love can also be cause for concern. If your dog is a dumpster diver or gets into a great cache of leftovers, he may be rewarded with a case of pancreatitis. Most veterinarians will tell you that they see a lot of pancreatitis cases around the holidays. The classic problem is that the dog gets into the Thanksgiving turkey, gorges on it, and then gets very sick.

The signs of pancreatitis include vomiting, diarrhea, and abdominal pain. Dogs with pancreatitis tend to stand in a characteristic "hunched over" position because of the pain. Dogs who get pancreatitis are often hospitalized and receive a course of fluids and antibiotics. Severe cases can be fatal.

A couple of traditional treats also are bad for pets. The traditional "give a dog a bone" idea isn't necessarily a good one. Although dogs love snacking on meat bones, the bone can splinter and puncture the stomach or intestines. Chicken and other poultry can be particularly dangerous as the bones become brittle when they are cooked. It's much safer to give your dog bones that are designed for pets.

It should go without saying, but giving your dog alcoholic beverages isn't funny. Most people are aware that too much alcohol can poison humans. Remember that your dog is a lot smaller than you are, so even small amounts of alcohol can be toxic. Pay attention at parties where pets may be able to get into drinks. If you smell alcohol on the animal's breath or notice behavioral changes, call the vet as soon as possible. Alcohol toxicity can be fatal.

Another obvious point is to keep your garbage in tightly covered garbage cans. Both cats and dogs often enjoy the challenge of getting into the garbage and seeing what leftovers they can find. Spoiled food can make a dog sick, the same way it can make you sick. A midnight run to the emergency vet clinic with your vomiting canine is probably not the way you want to spend your holidays.

Pet Proofing the Holidays

Animals tend to find all those special holiday items fun to play with or explore. Don't let your holiday turn into a tragedy. Every year veterinarians treat animals for electrocution, ingestion of foreign objects, burns, cuts from broken glass, and poisoning from toxic plants or chemicals.

Think about how you can pet proof the following:

Christmas Tree: Pets may knock it over, so you can either keep it in a room that can be closed off or put a barrier around it, such as baby gates or a portable kennel fence (this can help keep kids safe too).

Pine needles can cause gastrointestinal distress for your pets, so don't let them chew up or eat the needles that will inevitably end up on the floor. Sweep up regularly and put a big sheet around the base of the tree, so when you take the tree out at the end of the season, you don't get needles everywhere.

If you have a puppy, be very sure to keep him away from electrical cords. Puppies and even kittens often like to chew on wires, so be sure all wires are out of critter range. You also can spray bitter apple spray on the cords as a deterrent.

Plants: A number of holiday plants are poisonous to pets, including holly, mistletoe, and poinsettia. Make sure they are placed where your pets can't get to them.

Ornaments/decorations: Tinsel, glass ornaments, electrical cords, and various edible decorations all can cause problems if they are ingested. Make sure they are secured so animals cannot get to them. Also keep food ornaments like popcorn strings off the lower branches. It's food, and your dog knows it.

Food: chocolate, alcohol, and caffeine can make pets very ill, or even kill them in some cases. Do not give your pets any holiday food and keep platters of goodies out of their reach.

Finally, know your dog. Some animals will eat absolutely any object they find on the floor, which results in an expensive vet trip to remove the object. If you have a dog like this, be extra careful about ornaments, ribbons, tinsel, presents, and holiday food. I know someone whose dog had emergency surgery to remove glass after the dog knocked a casserole on the floor and ate the dish along with the food.

Even though you may be really busy, the bottom line is: pay attention to your pets. With a little extra awareness and forethought on your part, you, the tree, and all your pets can make it through the holidays safely.

LETO

Tannenbaum Bomb

With six animals living in our house, every year, we ponder the realities of all that furry activity versus the Christmas tree. Maybe I've watched too many home videos on TV of pets toppling over trees, but I don't trust my critters around a lovely pine covered with fragile ornaments. We refer to Leto as "Clod Boy," and my cats' klutzy leaps have resulted in broken glassware more than once. So it's not exactly hard to imagine the sounds of yuletide destruction (i.e., a Tannenbaum Bomb).

Fortunately, because of the layout of our house and our vigilant furry critter supervision, we've managed to avoid massive tree devastation. Although an enterprising cat or dog can still take out a tree, here are a few things we've learned to keep the tree upright and all the ornaments intact.

The first thing is to pick a good place for the tree. If you have a room that can be closed off at night or while you aren't able to keep an eye on your pets, that's ideal. Alternatively, you can put up some kind of fence or blockade around the bottom of the tree to keep wagging tails and cats out of range. We use baby gates across the doorway to our sunroom where we keep the tree and just close it off completely at night. Although we haven't tried it, another way to keep the tree upright is to secure it to the wall or ceiling. Some people use strong fishing line attached to a hook in the ceiling. The line is invisible, and even if a pet tries to climb it, the tree should still stay upright.

Place plastic, wood, or other reasonably unbreakable ornaments at the bottom of the tree (where ornaments are most likely to be wagged off). We have a whole collection of rather ugly ornaments that we put low on the tree. Broken glass isn't fun for anyone.

Dog FAQ

When your dog's tail wags furiously at the sight of the postal carrier, are you sure she's delighted to see him? Or when she raises her paw, is she really trying to "shake hands?" And why would your dog eagerly eat grass... only to vomit it up almost immediately?

In this section, I answer some of the questions we've all asked, like "do dogs dream" and "why does my dog eat grass?"

Why Do Dogs Chase Their Tails?

Most dog owners have watched as their dog suddenly and for no apparent reason, notices the long appendage attached to that canine rear end. The dog glares at the offending tail for a moment and then goes after it in a great whirling production that often ends up with the dog in a pile on the floor with the tail in his mouth. Mission accomplished. But what exactly was the mission in the first place?

Dogs chase their tails for a number of reasons, some physical and some behavioral. A dog may chase his tail if he is itchy, has fleas, or is having anal gland problems. Basically anything causing distress in the rear half of the hound can instigate a tail chasing moment.

Some dogs receive positive reinforcement for tail chasing from their humans and may repeat the process to get attention. I mean, let's face it, tail chasing can be quite a hilarious performance and most dogs love to make people laugh.

Unfortunately, this seemingly harmless activity can have a darker side as well. In extreme cases, a dog may chase his tail so frequently that it's considered a form of obsessive-compulsive disorder. One theory is that tail chasing is a way to alleviate stress if the dog is feeling unsure about a situation. As with many stress-induced disorders, the dog may be displacing his anxiety about something in his life into a different activity. Big events such as a move or a new addition to the family could stimulate an increase in tail chasing, for example. If stress is at the root of the behavior, it may occur in conjunction with other obsessive-compulsive disorders, such as flank or paw licking, pacing, or circling.

Tail chasing behavior is more common in certain breeds than others. Some dogs can go their entire lives without chasing their tails, and some do it occasionally seemingly just to amuse themselves. Many times tail chasing begins in adolescent dogs and subsides as they get older, as if they've "grown out of it."

Unfortunately, dogs that bite and snap at their tails can actually injure themselves. Most behaviorists recommend spending more time with the dog and increasing the amount of exercise the dog gets (after all, a tired dog will be sleeping, not chasing his tail). You might take your dog for long walks, play fetch, or get involved in "dog sports" like flyball or agility.

In severe cases, anti-anxiety medications are used to treat problem tail-chasing behaviors. So if your dog's interest in his tail has gone a little too far lately, it's probably time to take him to the vet for a checkup.

How Old is Your Dog?

When you adopt a dog, sometimes even your veterinarian can't really conclusively tell you how old the dog actually is. With puppies, you can get a good idea of their age by looking at their teeth. Puppy baby teeth are replaced with adult teeth by 6 months old. After that, vets usually look at the amount of tartar and tooth wear to estimate a dog's age. Unfortunately, tartar can depend on food and even the environment the dog was exposed to as a youngster. Like people, some dogs just have really bad teeth, so determining their age can be a challenge.

The old adage about each year of a dog's age being equal to 7 human years isn't really true. For example, a 1-year-old dog is roughly like a 12-year-old kid. A 2-year-old dog corresponds to a 22-year-old human. Anyone who has ever owned a dog would have to agree that canine adolescence can range anywhere from about 7 or 8 months to 2 or 3 years old. Dogs reach middle age around 6, which is equivalent to a 45-year-old human. At 10, she's like a 65-year-old; at 13, an 80-year-old; and at 15, like a 90-year-old.

A few obvious signs indicate that your dog is a senior citizen. Depending on the breed of dog, you may notice that her muzzle starts to go gray. Of course if you have a white dog, you won't see that clue. And some dogs actually go prematurely gray, just like humans do.

Many older dogs also get a type of cloudiness in their eyes. This condition is a hardening of the lens protein and is not the same thing as cataracts. Although it may look somewhat like cataracts, the dog can still see. However, if you notice that your dog's eyes look cloudy, you should check with your veterinarian.

In general, it's a good idea to keep a close eye on your canine friend as she ages. Some illnesses become more likely as dogs age. Often many of these diseases can be treated, which can improve your dog's quality of life in her senior years.

Some dogs do live a lot longer than others. No one knows how long a particular dog will live, but certain genetic predisposition to disease may shorten a dog's life span. For example, many Cavalier King Charles spaniels have a genetic problem with mitral valve disease, so they often don't live as long as other medium-sized dogs.

In general, the life span of a dog goes up as the size goes down. Giant breeds like Great Danes age faster than Chihuahuas. Because giant breeds live 7–10 years, they actually are considered "geriatric" starting as early as 4 years old. Conversely, small breeds can live up to 18 years.

If you have a mutt, you can guess her life span by considering the approximate breed makeup and size. But no matter how long your "best friend" lives, it probably won't be long enough.

Do Dogs Dream?

Research confirms what pretty much every dog owner knows: dogs dream when they sleep, just like people do. I can attest that my dog Tika, the golden retriever, has a very active dream life. It appears that she runs, woofs, squeaks, wiggles, and eats while asleep.

Dogs have different phases of sleep, just like humans do. The only difference is in the length of time. Our sleep cycles tend to be longer, but like people, dogs go through slow wave sleep (SWS) and rapid eye movement (REM) sleep. All that dreaming happens in the REM sleep cycle.

When your dog is still and breathing deeply, he's probably in the SWS sleep phase. Although he seems to be doing a great imitation of a rug, he's actually much more likely to wake up during this sleep phase than during REM sleep. Once the dog starts "running" or twitching, he's in the REM cycle, which is extremely deep sleep and when tests have shown there is the most brain activity.

Apparently a dog's sleep position also indicates how they sleep. A dog curled up in a tight ball may look like he's sleeping hard, but may not be. To enter the deepest REM sleep a dog has to be completely relaxed. But he can't be completely relaxed when all his muscles are tensed to keep him curled up. So that compact hound may be more awake than you thought.

Along the same lines, a dog sleeping on his back with his feet in the air isn't doing it just to be weird. Dogs have less fur on their tummies, so when they are hot, they tend to sleep upside-down, since it cools them off.

And here's one I always suspected. Dogs who lie back to back are bonding with one another. When they lie with their back resting on you, they are bonding with you. This contact shows a desire to be with the other dog or human. It's a way of showing affection.

Interestingly, puppies and old dogs dream more than middle-aged dogs. So as your dog ages, you can expect more dream activity. This change also may be part of why older dogs may seem to be more irritable. Dogs that are awakened from deep REM sleep may respond in much the same way you do: grouchily. In fact, it's important to instill in kids that old adage: "let sleeping dogs lie."

Statistically, 60 percent of dog bites happen to children, and 70 percent of dog bites occur on the owner's property. In other words, the family dog can and will bite the kid if the kid hasn't been taught how to behave around the family pet. Although it's fun to watch the antics of dreaming dogs, it's best to let them dream their happy dreams of chasing squirrels uninterrupted.

Why Do Dogs Eat Grass?

For a long time, I thought my dogs ate grass because their stomachs were upset. Over time, I've realized that they seem to eat grass pretty much any old time. They are just grazing fools.

But it still makes you wonder, so why do dogs eat grass anyway? Pretty much every dog I've ever owned has munched down on the lawn like a furry sheep at one time or another. Considering dogs are primarily meat-eaters, it seems like an odd activity.

After researching this question in many books and online, I've learned that no one seems to know why dogs eat grass. People have a lot of theories however. The idea that I heard years ago (from my Mom actually) is that the dog feels queasy and knows he has eaten something disgusting. So he eats grass to make his tummy feel better. You have Tums; your dog has the lawn.

Other people suggest that since dogs often throw up after eating grass, maybe they are doing it on purpose. The dog feels sick, so to make himself vomit, he snarfs down some grass. The grass irritates his stomach and he yaks everything up on the carpet. Given that so many dogs throw up after eating grass, I can definitely buy into that idea.

Another theory is that dogs need a balanced diet, so Rover is just making an effort to eat his veggies because today's dog food doesn't include enough nutrition. Dogs are descended from wolves and a related theory says that dogs are after vegetable matter because it's historically been part of their diet. When wolves kill something and eat it, they get the stomach contents along with the meat. Since wolves eat a lot of herbivores, they get sort of second-hand plant material. Ancestors of dogs used to get lots of grasses this way, so dogs still like eating grass.

The consensus seems to be that unless your dog really goes nuts about it, eating grass is a normal activity for your furry friend, so you don't really need to worry about it. However, before you let your dog graze on the neighbor's lawn, make sure that the grass hasn't been sprayed with any type of chemicals, such as fertilizer, pesticides, or herbicides. Limit your dog's snacking to organically grown non-toxic greenery.

How Can I Have a Dog and a Job Too?

We've all seen (and usually heard) dogs left outside all day to fend for themselves or chained to a doghouse, presumably while their owners are at work. Less obvious are those dogs that are left at home all day trapped in a crate. Dogs are social animals and when they are left alone for hours every day, behavior problems may occur.

Because I work from home, my situation is ideal for my dogs. I can keep an eye on them and they can keep an eye on me. But even dogs that spend a lot of their time with their owners can end up with behavioral issues when the owner goes out. The self-employed do leave the house once in a while, and many years ago, one of our dogs expressed her displeasure at being left behind by chewing up the house.

Unfortunately, this type of destruction, barking, obsessive-compulsive behaviors, and anxiety are all potential results of social deprivation and boredom. Even though almost all dogs were bred to do some type of work, too many of them are forced to spend their days doing nothing at all. As with little kids, if you don't give a dog something to do, she will find something to do. And it will undoubtedly be something you won't like.

If you work all day, you also need to be fair to the dog. Dogs that are crate trained can spend time in their crate while you're gone, but it's cruel to leave a dog crated for hours on end. You wouldn't enjoy being trapped for more than four hours without bathroom privileges, and neither does your dog.

If you can't come home for lunch to let out your dog, find a pet sitting service, or ask a neighbor to do it for you. Professional "doggie day care" facilities are another option. If you can't find one and don't know anyone in the neighborhood, talk to a vet clinic or animal shelter and ask if they know any animal lovers. Many people who like dogs would welcome the opportunity to play with your dog in exchange for a few bucks. When I was growing up, my parents paid a neighborhood kid to stop by every day after school to let out the dogs. While they were outside, she ate Oreos and watched TV for a while. Everyone was happy.

Owning a dog when you have a job is not impossible. But when you're home, be sure to give your dog lots of love and exercise. After all, a tired dog is a good dog.

LEIA

Top 10 Reasons Dogs are Better Office Mates than Humans

I share my office space with four dogs. Over the years, I've worked in offices with humans and dogs and I've decided that dogs are much easier to work with. Here's my list of the top 10 reasons dogs are better office mates than humans.

10. Dogs don't spend all day surfing eBay or questionable Web sites that play stupid music.

9. Dogs can't whistle while they work.

8. Dogs don't like speakerphones. It's okay if you're talking, but if someone else is talking back through the speaker, it needs to be woofed at to tell it to shut up.

7. Dogs like quiet. The sound of typing is soothing to them and helps them sleep.

6. Dogs don't judge you by how much money you make and aren't jealous of your salary. If you make enough to pay for the dog food, everything is fine.

5. Dogs know that when you say "no," you really mean it. They don't go talk to your manager.

4. Dogs are trainable. You don't have to explain the organizational chart more than once. (If you want the dog chow tonight, I'm the CEO.)

3. Dogs don't criticize your work.

2. Dogs don't care what you are wearing. They think the concept of "dressing for success" is stupid. Dogs like it when you wear comfortable shoes because they make better pillows than high heels.

And the number one reason dogs make better office mates:

1. Dogs never schedule "informational" meetings. They can't talk and "when is dinner?" doesn't require a meeting notice.

....

What is The "Human–Animal Bond"?

If you love animals, you may have read about the "human–animal" bond. The American Veterinary Medical Association policy defines it as: "a mutually beneficial and dynamic relationship between people and animals that is influenced by behaviors that are essential to the health and well-being of both. This includes, but is not limited to, emotional, psychological, and physical interactions of people, animals, and the environment. The veterinarian's role in the human–animal bond is to maximize the potentials of this relationship between people and animals."

In other words, having pets makes you feel good, both physically and mentally.

Many medical studies have shown that pet owners have lower stress levels and fewer heart attacks. If you have a dog or cat, you always have someone to come home to and your furry friend will never tell your boss all the horrible things you said after a particularly bad day at the office. It should come as no surprise that researchers have found that petting and talking to a companion animal actually reduces blood pressure.

Many people have told me that if they had unlimited space and money, they'd have more pets. I probably would too. But why do people feel so strongly about their pets? Realistically, having pets is a lot of work. I've never seen a scientific explanation why people find pets so appealing. I mean, why is a puppy adorable, even when he's eating your shoe? Why does seeing a cat snoring in a windowsill make you smile?

The bond that forms between a pet and his humans often happens quickly. Even if a person has only had a pet a few weeks, if the pet gets sick, it can be traumatic because the attachment has already formed. The bond increases over time and people often sink into terrible depression after the death of a pet.

You see your pets every day for 10–15 years. That's a lot more than many people see their relatives, so it's no surprise to feel great loss when your pet is gone. Pet loss support hotlines have become more widely available. In the past, people seemed to think that it wasn't okay to grieve for "just a dog" or "just a cat," but these days you can even buy pet loss sympathy cards.

Many retirement facilities and hospitals bring in pets for visits or have a pet at the facility. Animal assisted therapy is being used for more health issues than ever before. Guide dogs continue to help the blind, but now assistance dogs also help deaf humans, the physically handicapped, and people with epilepsy, Parkinson's disease, and other afflictions. In fact, a recent article in Tuft's "Your Dog" newsletter described how an assistance dog is helping an autistic girl control her repetitive actions. In the past, the girl would run and scream in stressful situations, but with the help of her assistance dog, she can now sit quietly and relate better to people.

It's just more proof that the human–animal bond is special. Every pet is different, but the bond is there.

How Can I Say Goodbye?

For many people, the dogs and cats in the household are part of the family. Because of the relatively short life spans of pets, at some point, almost all pet owners must make some difficult decisions and then deal with the loss of a pet. Unfortunately, society often isn't understanding about the feelings of grief people experience when a pet dies. Clichés and sometimes unhelpful advice may make the grieving process more difficult than it has to be. If you viewed your dog as a friend, it's not fair for people to judge your feelings and say, "he was just a dog." The reality is that it's not stupid for you to miss your dog, and you aren't being a "sentimental fool" for grieving for your lost pet.

The decision to euthanize your dog may also complicate the grieving process. When a dog is suffering or unlikely to recover, euthanasia is often decided upon to end a pet's pain. Although this decision is difficult, people need to recognize that sometimes this is the kindest thing we can do for our dogs in the final stages of their life. Sometimes understanding more about the process of euthanasia can make the decision less painful. Talk to your veterinarian about what is involved. Some vets will come out to your home, which may be less stressful for you and the dog. Some people may feel they need to be with the dog during the final moments; some do not. Either way, you shouldn't feel guilty for all the things you "should have done."

After your dog is gone, realize that there will be a gap in your life. Some people think they "hear" their pet in the yard or at the door or have dreams about their lost dog. Grief is a process that can be very difficult to work through. It takes time.

Especially if you have kids, be sure to talk about their feelings. Kids deserve time to accept the loss too, so don't rush out and get another dog. That can give the impression that the dog that died wasn't special. Of course, it's a lot easier to write about this topic than to experience it. There's no way to really completely prepare yourself for the loss of a treasured friend.

Intellectually, we all know that dogs and cats generally only live about 15 years at the most, yet I know that no matter how much I may prepare myself, when the inevitable happens and one of my pets dies, I'll be a basket case.

It's All Worth It

Although you will undoubtedly outlive your pets, that fact shouldn't keep you from enjoying life with a furry friend. I've actually met people that have decided never to own a dog or any other pet because saying goodbye is too "hard." But I think missing out on all those years of canine companionship is really sad.

I know that I'll always have dogs. I don't want to miss out on the joy of sharing my life and home with a goofy, happy hound. To me, that experience is what it's all about. Although Bingo, Shadow, Rufus, Toby, and Judge are no longer in my life, I'm blessed with thousands of memories of the time I shared with them. I wouldn't trade that for anything.

If you've read through all the sidebars in this book, you know that adopting my current madcap canine crew hasn't always been easy. But I know I saved their lives, and in the process, also immeasurably enriched my own.

May your dogs make you as happy as Leia, Tika, Cami, and Leto have made me.

Index

A

accidents 80, 83
acral lick dermatitis 159
acute moist dermatitis 159
adjusting to new experiences 54
adolescence 94
adopting a dog 1–26
  finding 21
  from a shelter 17
  from breed rescue 18
  holidays 22
  is it right for you? 11
  options 16
  why adopt? 8
affection 183
  demanding 66
age 180
aggression 93, 115
alarm barking 107
alcohol 174
allergies 131, 158
alpha 39, 66
amitriptyline 142
anal glands 179
anesthesia 147
animal abuse 10
animal shelter 11, 116
  reasons for relinquishing dogs 13
  visiting 16
antibiotics 130
antifreeze 161, 163, 171
anxiety 92, 112, 115, 152, 180

arthritis 155, 170
attention 74

B

baby gate 37, 114
bacterial infection 129, 145
barking 107, 185
bathing 31, 126
bed 28, 30
　go to command 79
begging 97
behavior 43, 52
　problems 89–122
　reinforcing 63
behaviorist 41, 93, 117, 159
beta 39
bite 183
　prevention 57
biting 115, 158
bloat 152
blood work 140
blowing coat 135
boarding kennel 145
body language 45
bond 10, 183
　human-animal 1, 188
　with rescued dog 31
bones 174
bordetella 144
boredom 52, 107, 185
boundaries 66
bowls 27
brain chemistry 116
brain tumor 157
breathing 152
breed 48
　checklist 15

  choosing 13
  mixed 14
  rescue 18
breeding 35
bricks 102
bringing home your dog 27–42
bromide 157
brushing 124, 134
  teeth 147
burn 169, 174
burrs 125
buying supplies 27

C

cage crazy 116
calling dog 73
calm 97
Cami 6, 50, 78, 119, 141, 166, 169
car 164
carpet rake 134
cataracts 181
cats 37
chain 75
changes
  adapting to 55
  life 92
chasing
  cars 99
  cats 37
  tail 179
chemicals 85
chewing 114, 147, 148
children 38
  safety 58
chocolate 162, 173
choke chain 75
choosing

breed 13
  veterinarian 137
Christmas tree 177
cigarettes 162
cleanings
  teeth 147
clean up 84
climbing fences 101
clippers 125
Clomicalm 142
coat 14
cold 168, 170
collar 28
  flat buckle 29
comb 125
coming home 97
commands 53, 60
  come 73
  down 71
  go to your bed 79
  housebreaking 82
  release word 71
  sit 67
communication 43, 48, 53
cone. *See* E-collar
confidence 104
confining 100
consistency 44, 60
convulsions 156, 163
correction 65
costs of dog ownership 12
cowering 104
crate 28, 80, 81, 85, 186
cue 71

D

"doggie" odor 129

day care 186
death 190
dehydration 154
dental care 146
Deramaxx 156
destabilizing pack order 40
destructive chewing 114
diabetes 106, 117
diarrhea 117, 154, 163
digging 102, 108
Dirofilaria immitis. *See* heartworm
disease 144
  Lyme 155
distemper 144
divorce 92
dog
  and children 32
  bowls 27
  breeds
    checklist 15
    choosing 13
    mixed 14
    rescue groups 18
  door 168
  food 28
doghouse 168
dominance 39, 43, 106
down 71
dreaming 182
drying dog 127
dynamics
  pack 66

E

E-collar 149, 150
ears 47, 131
  infection 159

eating
  non-food items 117
  poisonous substances 163
education 53–88
electrocution 174
Elizabethan collar. *See* E-collar
enzymatic cleaner 84
escaping 101
estimating age 181
ethylene glycol. *See* antifreeze
EtoGesic 156
euthanize 190
exam
  yearly 139
excitement 97
  urination 106
exercise 51, 123
experiences 27, 54
exposure to new things 55
eye contact 106
eyes 181

F

family
  adjusting 36
  violence 10
fat 143
fear
  loud noises 110, 167
fearfulness 56, 104, 107
feeding 32, 44
feline 37
fence jumping 101
fever 154
finding
  lost dog 102
  veterinarian 137

fire 169
fireworks 167
flank sucking 159
fleas 132, 179
follower 44
food 28
  motivation 61
food allergy 158
Fourth of July 167
free dogs 21
frostbite 171
full-body shake 128
fur 14, 123

G

garage door openers 162
garbage 174
gastric dilatation and volvulus. *See* bloat
Gentle Leader 75
getting a dog
  should you? 12
go to your bed 79
grass 184
Great Undercoat Removal Program 136
grief 190
grooming 121, 123
group names 42
growl 115
guillotine trimmer 130

H

hair 134
  long 14
  loss 158
harness 75
head halter 75
health 51, 123–160

heartworm 140, 151
heat stress 165
hepatitis 144
hierarchy 43
  pack 40, 66
hip dysplasia 155
holes 108
holidays 22, 153, 173
homecoming 97
homeopathic 112
hormone imbalances 106
hormones 116, 131
hot spots 159
hot weather 164
housebreaking 80
household hazards 163
human-animal bond 1, 10
Humane Society of the United States (HSUS) 57
hyperactivity 96, 98, 167, 172, 173

I

identification 28, 165
idiopathic seizure 157
immune system 144
inappropriate elimination 106
indoor poisonous plants 162
infection 144
  ear 131, 159
insecurity 89
intranasal vaccine 146
introducing 55
itching 159, 179
itchy skin 129

J

jealousy 93
job 185

joint pain 155
July Fourth 167
jumping 95

K

keeping your dog healthy 123–160
keeping your dog safe 161–178
kennel cough 144
kids 38
  safety 58

L

leadership 40, 43, 60, 72, 75
learn to earn 69, 89
leash 28, 29
  walking 75
Leia 4, 42, 120, 150, 160, 187
leptospirosis 144
Leto 7, 113, 128, 141, 177
lick granuloma 142
licking 120, 158, 180
life span 190
lifestyle
  changes 11
lint brush 135
litter 35
long down 71
lost dogs 102
low blood sugar 157
Lyme disease 155
lymphocytic plasmacystic enteritis 141

M

mad ears 47
manners 53, 59, 96
  mouth 56
marking 109

master 44
mats 124
medicine 140
medium chain triglycerides 141
mentality
  pack 43
metronidazole 141
miracle of birth 35
mood 48
motivation 61, 63, 74
mouthing 56
multiple dogs 32
Murphy's Law 119

N

nails 130
National Dog Bite Prevention week 57
Nature's Miracle 84, 110
nausea 163
neighbors 100
neurological problems 156
nipping 56
no
  saying 65
no-pull harness 77
noise 110, 167
nonsteroidal anti-inflammatory drugs 156
nothing in life is free. *See* learn to earn
nuisance 96
nutrient deficiency 117

O

obedience training 53
obesity 143, 155
  human 51
obsessive-compulsive 121, 159, 180, 185
odors 84

office 187
okay 68, 73
omega 39
ornaments 175
outdoor poisonous plants 162
overfeeding 66
overheating 165
overweight 143

P

pack 36, 39
  leader 40, 43, 60, 66, 72
  order 39
pain 116, 154
pancreatitis 153, 173
parainfluenza 144
paralysis 163
parasites 131
parking 164
parking lot pups 20
parvovirus 144
patience 11, 94
patio blocks 102
pedicure 130
perfect dogs 1
personality tests 23
pesticides 165, 185
pet ownership
  health benefits 10
pet sitter 186
pH 126
phenobarbital 157
phobia 112
physicals 139
pica 117
plants
  poisonous 162, 175

plastic bowls 27
play bow 45
poisoning 157, 174
poisonous plants 162
pool 166
positive reinforcement 62, 179
post-surgical care 148
pregnancy 36
preventative
  heartworm 151
prey drive 37
problems
  flea 133
  people 91
prophylaxis 147
proud 48
pulling 75
puppy
  proofing 114, 161
  socialization 54
purebred rescue 19
put to sleep 190

Q

quick 131

R

rabies 144
rain 168
reading a dog 48
rebellion 94
reinforcement 64
relationship 1, 40, 90
release word 68, 70, 73
REM sleep 182
rescue 18
  darker side 19

respect 59
response 64
restlessness 152
retrieving 51
reward-based training 62
Rimadyl 156
roaming dogs 99
rocks 117
rolling over 45
rug rake 134
rules 44, 59, 66, 90
running away 99

S

safety 161–178
salivating 152
saying "no" 65
schedule
  housebreaking 82
scratching 158
seizures 156
self-mutilation 158
separation anxiety 107, 114
shake 127
shampoo 126
shedding 134, 136
shelter 11, 116
  visiting 16
shyness 56, 90, 104
sit 67, 90
  releasing 70
  stomp 69
skin 158
  irritation 123
  problem 129
sky kennel 28, 81
sleep 182

slicker brush 125
slow wave sleep 182
slurping 160
snap 115
snow 168, 172
socialization 36, 54
sore 121
spay and neuter 9, 33, 94, 110, 116, 165
  early age 34
spoiled 65
stainless steel bowls 27
stains 84
stay vs. okay 70
stiffness 155
stinky dog 129
stitches 149
storms 110
stress 9, 105, 159, 188
structure 89
stubbornness 78
submissive 39, 45, 120
  urination 105, 142
summer 164
supplies 27
surgery 148

T

table scraps 155
tail 48
  chasing 159, 179
  wagging 45
tangled hair 125
teaching sit 67
teen 94
teeth 146, 181
temperament test 23
test

  personality 23
Thanksgiving turkey 153
theobromine 173
thirst 163
thunder 113
thunderstorms 110
thyroid 106, 116, 157
Tika 5, 69, 98, 172
time 11
timing
  in training 62
toes 172
top dog. *See* alpha
toxic substances 161
toys 28
training 53–88
  come 73
  down 71
  go to your bed 79
  housebreaking 80
  misconceptions 61
  sit 67
  walking on a leash 75
trees 78
trimming nails 130

U

understanding 43–52
urinary tract infections 106
urination 163
  marking 109
  submissive 105
urine 84

V

vaccinations 144
vacuum 104

vehicle 164
veterinarian
  choosing 137
veterinary exam 139
viral disease 144
vocalization 50
vomiting 117, 152, 154, 163, 173

W

wagging 45
walking 51, 102
  on a leash 75
washing 126
weakness 163
weight
  losing 143, 168
weighted bowl 27
what's in it for me. *See* positive reinforcement
whining 152
winter 168, 170
woo 50
wood stove 169
work 185

Y

yearly exam 139
yeast infection 129

About the Author
Susan Daffron

Susan Daffron is the President of Logical Expressions, Inc. a publishing company in Sandpoint, Idaho. She also has been a veterinary assistant and worked at animal shelters as an employee and volunteer. She currently owns four dogs and two cats, all of whom came from animal shelters or rescues

Susan has written more than 70 articles that have appeared in national magazines, more than 200 newspaper articles, an online software training course, a software book, cookbook, and book chapters.

In addition to her writing experience, Susan has more than 15 years of experience as a writer, editor, and designer of magazines, newsletters, books and other book-length documents such as users guides and manuals.

She publishes a popular weekly computing ezine called Logical Tips (http://www.logicaltips.com) and for two years published a free (print) computer "how to" magazine, which is archived at http://www.computorcompanion.com . The magazine has evolved into a quarterly and continues to receive rave reviews from online computer users.

Susan also publishes a pet ezine called Pet Tails that comes out two times/month. She has written more than 200 articles for this pet care site (http://www.pet-tails.com). She also publishes an ezine about Sandpoint Idaho (http://www.sandpointinsider.com) and articles for a newsletter site called Newsletter Help (http://www.newsletterhelp.com).

Share Happy Hound with a Friend

If you like this book, share it with your dog-loving friends!

Order Form

Please send me:

Qty	Title	Price	Total
	Happy Hound: Develop a Great Relationship with Your Adopted Dog or Puppy	$19.95	
	Shipping & Handling - $4.50 for first book, $1.00 for each additional book for US Priority Mail within the U.S.*		

_____ Check enclosed with order

_____ Please charge my credit card   [   ] Visa   [   ] Master Card

Number: _____

Name on Card: _____ Exp. Date: _____

Buyer's Name:_____

Buyer's Address: _____

Shipping Address (if different):_____

_____

Please fax to 208-265-0956 or mail with your payment to:

Logical Expressions, Inc.
311 Fox Glen Road, Sandpoint, ID 83864

*   *Please contact us for more information on orders mailed outside of the U.S.*
    (Our number is 208-265-6147)

Breinigsville, PA USA
04 October 2009
225204BV00001B/9/A